A TASTE OF

THE *Loveless Cafe*

100+
DOWN-HOME RECIPES *for*
SOUTHERN ENTERTAINING

WRITTEN BY BO MORRIS

PHOTOS BY PHILLIP FRYMAN

STORY FARM

A Taste of the Loveless Cafe
Copyright © 2021 by The Loveless Cafe
www.lovelesscafe.com

Photographs copyright © 2021 Phillip Fryman
www.SouthernFatty.com

Published in the United States by Story Farm
www.story-farm.com

All rights reserved. No portions of this book may be reproduced in any form without the written consent of The Loveless Cafe and Story Farm.

Library of Congress-Cataloging-in-Publication Data available upon request.
ISBN 978-1-7376046-0-0

Editorial director	Bo Morris
Art director	Jason Farmand
Copy editor	Laura Paquette
Production manager	Tina Dahl
Food stylist	Callie Blount
Project managers	The Loveless Cafe Marketing and Culinary Teams

---

Printed in Canada by Friesens Corporation

First printing, November 2021
10 9 8 7 6 5 4 3 2 1

This book is dedicated to all of our guests over the past seven decades who have celebrated milestones and made lifelong memories while enjoying a meal around a table at the Loveless Cafe.

CONTENTS

Introduction	9
BREAKFAST & BISCUITS	14
DRESSINGS & SPREADS	42
APPETIZERS & DIPS	52
SUPPER	70
SIDES	98
DRINKS	120
DESSERTS	136
Index	171

Introduction

Here at the Loveless Cafe, fried chicken and biscuits are our jam, and we've been making perfect batches of both since 1951, when Lon and Annie Loveless began feeding hungry travelers out of their home nestled along the serene Natchez Trace Parkway. Word of their Southern hospitality and must-try chicken and biscuits soon spread far and wide, prompting Lon and Annie to convert their house into a restaurant, add a 14-room motel, a smokehouse, and expand the menu to include their now famous country ham and scratch-made preserves.

Nowadays, we're still frying chickens and baking a whole lot of biscuits, to the tune of around 10,000 biscuits per day. We've had the honor of serving our Southern staples to all kinds of famous folks like Taylor Swift, Dolly Parton, Al Gore, and even Paul McCartney, who famously sang an impromptu version of "Happy Birthday" to a guest at a nearby table who was celebrating turning 16.

You don't have to be famous to pull up a chair and enjoy delicious down-home vittles at one of our red-checkered tablecloths though. The Loveless Cafe attracts nearly half-a-million visitors a year from all walks of life and corners of the world, who appreciate classic comfort food served by the smiling faces that have greeted our diners for the past seven decades.

One of those gracious grins forever enshrined in the Loveless legacy belonged

to Carol Fay Ellison, aka "The Biscuit Lady." During her 30 years in the kitchen, Carol Fay was the face of the Loveless Cafe—and the voice, too. It was impossible to visit without hearing Carol Fay's infectious laugh or catching her mid-story as she passionately rolled out dough for another batch of those beloved biscuits. She also helped bring national attention to our humble Nashville home. When Willard Scott came to town to film an episode of NBC's Today Show in 2005, Carol Fay appeared on live TV alongside him, with Scott proclaiming Loveless Cafe makes "the world's greatest scratch biscuits." Martha Stewart, who proclaimed that the Loveless Cafe served the "best breakfast I ever had,"

INTRODUCTION

most exciting nights in our history, our team prepared a highly acclaimed "Loveless Valentine's Dinner" for a group of New York City's culinary elite featuring some of the signature Southern dishes responsible for making Loveless Cafe one of the country's favorite dining destinations.

After nearly 70 years that included a few facelifts and touchups here and there, we've always managed to stay true to our Southern roots and committed to homemade cooking using from-scratch ingredients, a proud tradition that carries on from when Lon and Annie founded the Loveless Cafe. Our current owners are native Nashvillians intent on preserving the enduring legacy of the Loveless Cafe. While the motel is no longer operational, the historic rooms now house several onsite shops and the Harpeth Room for small private events. The Loveless Barn, the grand structure in the rear of our property, has been added for larger events. We've even gone mobile with the Loveless Cafe Food Truck, which can be spotted cruising around Nashville dishing out our Southern staples to festival goers, wedding parties, or just about any other type of social gathering with hungry mouths to feed.

The following pages share some of our most cherished recipes from over the years in hopes that home cooks can make delicious meals that spark lively conversations, serve up lots of laughter, and make lifelong memories with friends, family, and loved ones. Just like a meal at the Loveless Cafe. Does that mean we're finally sharing our secret biscuit recipe after all these years? Guess you'll just have to keep on reading to find out…

invited Carol Fay on her TV show to share some of her Southern cooking tips. Before passing away in 2010, Carol Fay met, mingled, and cooked with the likes of Paula Deen, Bobby Flay, Conan O'Brien, Ellen DeGeneres, and of course, the countless number of friends, family, and fans who visited her at the Loveless Cafe.

All the national attention helped earn us a coveted invitation to cook at the famed James Beard House in 2013. In one of the

Breakfast & Biscuits

BREAKFAST & BISCUITS

Red Velvet Waffles

MAKES 4 BELGIAN WAFFLES

We're big fans of red velvet anything. Such big fans that we designate February as Red Velvet Month at Loveless Cafe. These eye-popping waffles will surely start your day in a celebratory fashion.

- 1 bag Loveless Cafe Belgian Waffle and Pancake Mix
- 5 tablespoons cocoa powder
- 1/8 teaspoon cinnamon
- 1 2/3 cups water
- 1/4 cup buttermilk
- 3 tablespoons red food coloring
- 2 1/2 teaspoons vanilla extract
- Loveless Cafe Maple Syrup
- Whipped cream (optional)

Preheat waffle iron. Pour Waffle Mix into a large mixing bowl and sift in cocoa powder and cinnamon.

In a second bowl, stir together water, buttermilk, food coloring, and vanilla extract. Pour slowly into dry mixture. Once combined, let rest for 3 minutes.

Pour mixture into waffle iron in four batches, cooking per waffle iron directions. Top with Maple Syrup and fresh whipped cream.

BREAKFAST & BISCUITS

Chicken n' Waffles

SERVES 4

Here's a Southern staple that tastes just as good for breakfast as it does lunch or dinner. Made with our famous Fried Chicken Breading and Belgian Waffle Mix, this legendary Loveless Cafe pairing will have you licking your lips and going back for more!

MAKE FRIED CHICKEN

Rinse chicken pieces, then soak in cold, salted water for 30 minutes. Drain and pat dry.

Heat 1 inch of vegetable oil in a large skillet over medium-high heat (375 degrees in an electric skillet).

Place 2 cups Fried Chicken Breading into a mixing bowl.

Dredge chicken in the breading, coating well on all surfaces. Pat off excess breading and place chicken in hot oil, making sure pieces are not touching each other.

When chicken is browned (approximately 5 minutes), turn pieces over and reduce heat to medium. Cover and cook for 20 minutes.

Remove lid, increase heat to medium-high, and flip chicken. Cook an additional 5 to 7 minutes, until crispy and golden brown.

Remove chicken from grease and drain on a paper towel before serving.

MAKE WAFFLES

Preheat waffle iron. Prepare waffles according to package instructions.

ASSEMBLY

Place waffle on a large plate and top with one portion chicken. Drizzle the entire waffle and chicken with Maple Syrup or Old-Fashioned Sorghum.

FRIED CHICKEN

- 1 fryer chicken, 3 pounds or less, cut into 8 pieces
- 1 tablespoon salt
- Vegetable oil (for frying)
- 2 cups Loveless Cafe Fried Chicken Breading

WAFFLES

- 1 bag Loveless Cafe Belgian Waffle and Pancake Mix
- Loveless Cafe Maple Syrup
- Loveless Cafe Old-Fashioned Sorghum (optional)

Chocolate Chip Biscuits

MAKES APPROXIMATELY 40 BISCUITS

When you can't decide between savory or sweet, these Chocolate Chip Biscuits are the perfect treat. And while it might be frowned upon to eat chocolate chip cookies for breakfast, no one bats an eye if they are served in biscuit form. At least here at the Loveless Cafe we don't.

Ingredients

- 1½ cups unsalted butter, divided
- 1 bag Loveless Cafe Biscuit Mix
- ½ cup sugar
- 1 cup semi-sweet chocolate chips
- 2⅔ cups buttermilk
- 1 teaspoon vanilla
- 1 cup all-purpose flour

Instructions

Preheat oven to 400 degrees. Grease a baking sheet or your favorite cast iron skillet with butter.

In a large bowl, mix together Biscuit Mix, sugar, and chocolate chips. Fold in buttermilk and vanilla. Mix until a sticky dough is formed.

Place dough on a well-floured surface. Dust top of dough heavily with flour. Knead dough per package instructions.

Roll out dough to ½-inch thick with a floured rolling pin, adding flour to top of dough and rolling surface as needed to avoid sticking. Do not re-roll dough more than once.

Cut out biscuits with a 2-inch cutter. Place biscuits on baking sheet or skillet with the sides touching one another. Melt remaining butter. Brush biscuits with half of melted butter before baking.

Bake for 10 to 15 minutes, rotating once about halfway through until biscuits are a light brown color. Remove biscuits from oven and brush with melted butter one more time. Allow to cool slightly before serving.

Breakfast Pizza

MAKES 2 PIES, 10 INCHES EACH

This rise-and-shine dish stars our famous Loveless Cafe Biscuit Mix as the pizza dough. Make sure to set your alarm early for this one because when you start the day with pizza for breakfast, you know a great day lies ahead.

MAKE PIZZA DOUGH

Preheat oven to 375 degrees.

Prepare Biscuit Mix per package instructions.

Roll out dough as if you were making biscuits (½-inch thick) and make one large round biscuit (approximately 10 inches wide), using a pie plate or dinner plate as a guide.

Slide dough onto a sheet pan or pizza stone. Brush the top of dough with melted butter and bake for 15 to 20 minutes, rotating pan in the oven halfway through baking so it cooks evenly. Top of dough should be lightly browned and the middle cooked through.

MAKE SCRAMBLED EGGS

While dough is baking, whisk eggs in a large mixing bowl until yolks are well-blended. Melt cold butter in a medium skillet over medium-low heat and add eggs, stirring constantly for 2 to 3 minutes until just set. Remove from heat and set aside.

ASSEMBLE

Remove biscuit base from oven and allow to cool for 10 minutes. Once cooled, slice the large biscuit in half crosswise with a serrated knife to make two large biscuits.

Flip the top over, browned side down, onto a second pan. Spoon 1½ cups prepared sausage gravy onto the top of each biscuit, spreading it to the edges all the way around.

Add scrambled eggs, cheeses, jalapeños, onions, mushrooms, and bacon.

Bake for 10 minutes or until cheese is melted. Remove from oven and serve.

- ½ bag Loveless Cafe Biscuit Mix
- 1⅓ cups buttermilk
- 1 cup all-purpose flour
- 2 tablespoons butter, melted
- 12 eggs
- ½ tablespoon butter, cold
- 3 cups Sausage Gravy (see page 39)
- 3 cups Swiss cheese, shredded
- 3 cups cheddar cheese, shredded
- ½ cup jalapeños, diced, sautéed
- ½ cup red onions, julienned
- 2 cups mushrooms, sautéed
- 2 cups Loveless Cafe Applewood Smoked Country Bacon, cooked and crumbled

BREAKFAST & BISCUITS

Loveless Cafe Biscuits

SERVES YOU AND YOUR LOVED ONES

- 1 visit to the Loveless Cafe
- 2 cups coffee
- 3 pats butter
-   Preserves, honey, and old-fashioned sorghum syrup (to taste)
- 1 new tradition for you and your family!

We've been making our buttermilk biscuits with the same secret recipe since 1951, so please understand why we're not about to let that particular cat out of the bag. You can always try our Loveless Cafe Biscuit Mix or Heat n' Eat Biscuits at home—or come dine with us in Nashville and we'll serve 'em right up! Just follow this easy recipe for the real thing.

Come see us!

Experience for yourself everything that has made the Loveless Cafe a Nashville tradition since 1951.

Biscuit Beignets

SERVES A CROWD

It's like having a little bit of New Orleans right here in Nashville whenever we make these fluffy pillows of fried dough and powdered sugar. These beignets are made using our signature Loveless Cafe Biscuit Mix, which gives an unmistakable Southern twist to the world-famous French Quarter fritter. Serve them with a strong cup of coffee to start your day in true New Orleans fashion.

Prepare Biscuit Mix per package instructions. Roll out dough to ¼-inch thick. Cut into 1-inch strips, then cut diagonally.

Pour oil into a Dutch oven or cast iron skillet to a depth of 2 to 4 inches. Heat over medium-high to 350 degrees. Fry dough in batches, about 1 to 2 minutes on each side or until golden brown.

Drain on paper towels and dust generously with confectioners' sugar.

- 1 bag Loveless Cafe Biscuit Mix
- 2⅔ cups buttermilk
- 1 cup all-purpose flour
- Vegetable oil (for frying)
- 2 cups confectioners' sugar

Blue Cheese Biscuits

MAKES APPROXIMATELY 40 BISCUITS

A cheesy twist on our best-selling biscuits that's perfectly acceptable to eat any time of day.

- 1½ cups unsalted butter, melted, divided
- 1 bag Loveless Cafe Biscuit Mix
- 2⅔ cups buttermilk
- 1 cup all-purpose flour
- 2 cups blue cheese crumbles

Preheat oven to 400 degrees and grease a baking sheet or cast iron skillet with melted butter.

In a large bowl, add Biscuit Mix and fold in buttermilk. Mix until a sticky dough is formed.

Place dough on a well-floured surface. Dust top of dough generously with flour. Knead dough per package instructions. Roll out dough with a floured rolling pin, adding flour to top of dough and rolling surface as needed to avoid sticking. Roll to ½-inch thick. Sprinkle blue cheese evenly across dough and fold over, sandwiching blue cheese between layers of dough. Re-roll dough no more than one time.

Cut out biscuits with a 2-inch cutter. Place biscuits on prepared baking sheet with sides touching one another. Brush biscuits with half of melted butter before baking.

Bake for 10 to 15 minutes, rotating once halfway through until biscuits are a light brown color.

Remove biscuits from oven and brush with remaining melted butter one more time. Allow to cool slightly before serving.

Bacon Cheddar Scones

WITH GREEN ONIONS

MAKES APPROXIMATELY 20 SCONES

These savory scones could almost pass as a standalone meal given the copious amounts of crispy bacon, cheddar cheese, and green onions. Not only do they smell and taste great, but they also look beautiful on the table for any occasion.

Preheat oven to 350 degrees. Line a baking sheet with parchment paper or wax paper and set aside.

Blend together Biscuit Mix, brown sugar, and salt in a mixer bowl with a paddle attachment. Add butter and blend until mixture looks like fine granules (approximately 2 minutes). Add milk and blend until combined.

Remove dough from bowl and transfer to a well-floured working surface. Gently fold in bacon, cheddar cheese, and green onions. Roll out the dough to approximately 1-inch thick and cut into 20 triangles.

Place triangles on parchment-lined baking sheet 1 inch apart.

Bake for 20 to 25 minutes until golden brown.

1	bag Loveless Cafe Biscuit Mix
2/3	cup light brown sugar, packed
1/2	teaspoon salt
1	cup butter, cold and cubed
1	cup milk
1/2	cup all-purpose flour
1	cup Loveless Cafe Applewood Smoked Country Bacon, cooked and chopped
1	cup sharp cheddar cheese, shredded
1/2	cup green onions, finely chopped

Pumpkin Spice Biscuits

MAKES APPROXIMATELY 40 BISCUITS

This recipe adds festive fall flavor to our famous biscuits, making it the perfect reliever for pumpkin spice fever!

Preheat oven to 400 degrees and grease a baking sheet or cast iron skillet with melted butter.

Add ½ cup sugar and 1 tablespoon pumpkin pie spice to biscuit mix, then stir together in a large mixing bowl.

Follow package instructions to make biscuits, adding 1 teaspoon vanilla extract to buttermilk.

Place dough on a well-floured surface. Dust top of dough generously with flour. Knead dough per package instructions. Roll out dough with a floured rolling pin, adding flour to top of dough and rolling surface as needed to avoid sticking. Roll out to ½-inch thick.

Cut out biscuits with a 2-inch cutter. Place biscuits on prepared baking sheet with sides touching one another and brush tops with melted butter.

Mix remaining ⅛ cup sugar and 1 teaspoon pumpkin pie spice. Sprinkle over top of biscuits.

Bake for 10 to 15 minutes, rotating pan halfway through until biscuits are a light brown color.

Enjoy with a dollop of Sweet Potato Butter.

- ½ cup unsalted butter, melted, divided
- ⅝ cup sugar, divided
- 1⅓ tablespoons pumpkin pie spice, divided
- 1 bag Loveless Cafe Biscuit Mix
- 2⅔ cups buttermilk
- 1 teaspoon vanilla extract
- 1 cup all-purpose flour
- Loveless Cafe Sweet Potato Butter

BREAKFAST & BISCUITS

Maple Bacon Pancake Muffins
WITH MAPLE CREAM CHEESE FROSTING

MAKES 12 TO 16 MUFFINS

MAPLE CREAM CHEESE FROSTING

- 2 (8-ounce) blocks cream cheese, softened
- 4 tablespoons Loveless Cafe Maple Syrup
- 1 cup confectioners' sugar
- ½ teaspoon kosher salt

PANCAKE MUFFINS

- ¼ pound Loveless Cafe Maplewood Smoked Country Bacon
- 1 bag Loveless Cafe Belgian Waffle and Pancake Mix
- Non-stick baking spray
- ¼ cup sugar
- 3 tablespoons Loveless Cafe Maple Syrup

These magnificent muffins are a signature creation of the Loveless Events team—and one of their most popular recipes. With just the right amounts of Maple Syrup and Maplewood Bacon, they're the perfect balance of sweet and salty and guaranteed to go fast on any breakfast spread. So make a big batch because there will be a house full of early risers when these muffins are in the oven.

MAKE MAPLE CREAM CHEESE FROSTING

Using an electric mixer on medium speed, blend the cream cheese and Maple Syrup together, scraping sides of bowl until combined.

Slowly add confectioners' sugar and salt. Scrape sides of bowl 2 to 3 times until all ingredients are combined.

Chill for at least 1 hour before using.

Note: Use a pastry bag with a star tip to pipe the icing or cut the corner off a resealable plastic bag and use it to top the muffins.

MAKE PANCAKE MUFFINS

Cook bacon according to package instructions until crispy.

Once cooked, place bacon on a paper towel to drain. When bacon is cooled, cut into ½-inch pieces or smaller and set aside.

Preheat oven to 350 degrees.

BREAKFAST & BISCUITS

Prepare Pancake Mix according to package instructions.

While oven is preheating, chill pancake batter and allow to rest for approximately 5 minutes.

Coat inside of muffin pan with non-stick spray.

Lightly coat the oiled pan with sugar, making sure the bottoms and sides are coated, then shake off the excess.

Pour batter into the oiled and sugared muffin pans, filling each three-quarters full.

Bake for 10 to 15 minutes or until a toothpick comes out clean, then cool to room temperature.

Top each muffin with frosting.

Sprinkle tops of frosted muffins with bacon, and drizzle with approximately ½ teaspoon of Maple Syrup.

Maple Bacon Sticky Biscuits

MAKES 20-24 BISCUITS

CARAMEL

- 1 pound Loveless Cafe Maplewood Smoked Country Bacon
- 1 cup unsalted butter
- ½ cup bacon grease (reserve after cooking)
- 2 pounds brown sugar
- ¼ cup water
- ¼ cup Loveless Cafe Maple Syrup

BISCUITS

- 1 cup sugar
- 1½ cups raisins, craisins, or chocolate chips
- 3 tablespoons cinnamon
- 1 cup all-purpose flour
- 1 bag Loveless Cafe Biscuit Mix
- 2⅔ plus ¾ cups buttermilk

This recipe stars three Loveless Cafe signature products—Maplewood Bacon, Maple Syrup, and of course, our world-famous biscuits—all rolled up into one sticky pleasure.

MAKE CARAMEL

Preheat oven to 350 degrees. Grease two 9-by-13 pans or two 12-inch cast iron skillets and set aside.

Cook bacon according to package instructions. Reserve grease and set aside. Chop bacon once cool and divide into 4 equal portions.

In a medium pot, bring butter, bacon grease, brown sugar, water, and Maple Syrup to a boil, stirring until smooth. Set aside.

MAKE BISCUITS

In a small bowl, mix sugar, raisins, and cinnamon. Set aside.

On a large cutting board, place a sheet of parchment paper or wax paper and dust with flour. In a large mixing bowl, pour in Biscuit Mix and work out any lumps with your hands. Add 2⅔ cups buttermilk and blend until a sticky dough is formed.

Place half the biscuit dough on parchment paper. Dust liberally with more flour and fold the dough 2 to 3 times, adding more flour if necessary. Roll out dough into a 9-by-13 rectangle.

Continues on page 34

Maple Bacon Sticky Biscuits

CONTINUED FROM PAGE 32

Brush dough liberally with remaining buttermilk. Sprinkle half of raisin mixture and one-fourth of chopped bacon on dough, keeping one long edge of dough moist but free of mixture to allow roll to seal.

Carefully roll dough into a tight log then repeat steps with remaining dough.

Using a serrated knife, cut the rolls into ½-inch slices. Divide the caramel between the two greased pans. Sprinkle each pan with chopped bacon. Place biscuit slices in the mixture, nesting them into caramel and making sure they are not crowded in the pan.

Bake until golden brown, about 20 to 30 minutes.

SERVE

Immediately after removing from oven, carefully invert the pans onto serving platters. Enjoy while warm.

Cheddar Garlic Biscuits

MAKES 20 BISCUITS

These light, fluffy gems are great for dinner parties and make a scrumptious complement to any dish.

Preheat oven to 400 degrees.

In a large bowl, add Biscuit Mix, buttermilk, cheese, and 1 teaspoon garlic powder. Mix by hand to form a soft ball of sticky dough.

Place dough on a well-floured surface. Dust top of dough heavily with flour. Gently fold flour into dough 2 to 3 times. With a floured rolling pin, roll to ½-inch thick then cut out biscuits with a 2-inch cutter.

Grease pan or cast iron skillet with 1 tablespoon melted butter. Place biscuits into pan with the sides touching one another against the pan.

Melt remaining 4 tablespoons butter in a saucepan over low heat. Remove from heat and stir in ¼ teaspoon garlic powder and minced chives. Lightly brush biscuits with melted garlic butter before placing in oven.

Bake for 8 to 10 minutes on middle rack, then rotate and finish baking for 8 to 10 more minutes until biscuits turn light brown. Remove from oven and brush with remaining garlic butter.

Serve warm.

- 2½ cups Loveless Cafe Biscuit Mix
- 1⅓ cups buttermilk
- 1 cup sharp cheddar cheese, shredded
- 1¼ teaspoon garlic powder, divided
- ½ cup all-purpose flour
- 5 tablespoons salted butter, divided
- ½ tablespoon chives, minced

BREAKFAST & BISCUITS

Hashbrown Casserole
SERVES 8

This velvety blend of shredded potatoes, cheddar cheese, and sour cream is one of our most in-demand dishes at the Loveless Cafe. And for good reason—it's absolutely addictive! So keep this recipe close by because friends and family will be requesting it time and time again.

- 1 (30-ounce) bag frozen shredded hashbrown potatoes, thawed
- 1 yellow onion, chopped
- 2 cups cheddar cheese, shredded
- 1 (10-ounce) can cream of chicken soup
- 2 cups sour cream
- Salt (to taste)
- Ground black pepper (to taste)

Preheat oven to 375 degrees. Grease a 9-by-13 casserole dish and set aside.

In a large bowl, combine potatoes, onion, cheese, soup, sour cream, salt, and pepper. Pour mixture into casserole dish.

Bake uncovered for 30 to 45 minutes or until the top is golden brown. Let stand for at least 5 minutes before serving.

TIMESAVING TIP

To save time, our Heat n' Eat Hashbrown Casserole is always available on our website for homemade Southern cooking without the fuss.

BREAKFAST & BISCUITS

Red Eye Gravy
SERVES 4

Red Eye Gravy, also known as poor man's gravy or red ham gravy, is an instantly recognizable Southern staple. Some folks even throw in a little red pepper to make it redder. But with this recipe, you just mix everything in the skillet and generously pour over your ham and biscuits—or wherever you like it best.

- 1 pound Loveless Cafe Country Ham, approximately ¼-inch thick
- ½ cup black coffee
- 1 tablespoon brown sugar

In a cast iron skillet over medium heat, add ham slices and warm until the ham starts to juice. Flip ham and cook for approximately 3 minutes per side.

Remove ham and deglaze the skillet by adding coffee and brown sugar. Over medium-low heat, bring sauce to a slow boil, stirring occasionally.

Remove from heat and spoon sauce over ham (and everything else) before serving.

Sausage Gravy

SERVES 4

This savory Sausage Gravy is a natural companion for our biscuits. And it's just as tasty spooned over grits, mashed potatoes, or, well, just about anything. So you might want to make enough to serve with supper, too!

In a large skillet over medium heat, cook pork sausage until browned (approximately 10 to 15 minutes), stirring occasionally and crumbling pork into smaller pieces as it browns.

Add flour and cook for 5 minutes, stirring occasionally. Add milk to flour and sausage and bring to a simmer. While continuously whisking the sausage mixture, add salt, black pepper, and cayenne, then stir until gravy has thickened.

Serve immediately.

- ½ pound ground pork sausage
- 2 tablespoons all-purpose flour
- 1½ cups milk
- Salt (to taste)
- 1 teaspoon ground black pepper
- ½ teaspoon cayenne pepper

BREAKFAST & BISCUITS

Sweet Potato Pancakes
WITH SPICED PECANS AND PEACH PRESERVES BUTTER

MAKES 8–10 PANCAKES

We guarantee you've never tasted flapjacks quite like these. The spiced pecans add a nice texture and the Peach Preserves Butter is the perfect pancake topper.

PEACH PRESERVES BUTTER

- ½ cup Loveless Cafe Peach Preserves
- ½ pound unsalted butter, softened
- Pinch of sea salt

SWEET POTATO PANCAKES

- 1 bag Loveless Cafe Sweet Potato Pancake Mix
- ½ cup Loveless Cafe Spiced Pecans, chopped
- Loveless Cafe Maple Syrup (optional)

MAKE BUTTER

In a medium bowl, combine all ingredients and mix until smooth. Cover and refrigerate until ready to use.

MAKE PANCAKES

Preheat skillet over medium heat. Mix pancake batter per package instructions.

Add ¼ cup batter onto hot skillet in batches. Sprinkle 2 teaspoons chopped pecans onto each pancake before flipping and cook until golden brown on each side.

When pancakes are done, top with a spoonful of peach preserves butter and Maple Syrup.

Dressings & Spreads

DRESSINGS & SPREADS

Loveless Cafe Preserves

(BLACKBERRY, STRAWBERRY, AND PEACH)

EACH RECIPE MAKES 4 CUPS OR 2 (16-OUNCE) JARS

No trip to Loveless Cafe is complete without smothering a warm biscuit with our Preserves. That's why you'll always find a jar of this homemade goodness on every table. Just follow these simple recipes and your dining room table can always have a jar of it, too.

BLACKBERRY PRESERVES

- 4 cups blackberries (fresh or frozen)
- 1 cup sugar

Gently rinse the blackberries with cold water in a colander. Set colander in sink and let dry.

Place blackberries in a large pot with sugar. Let sit for 2 hours or until the berries release their juices.

Bring blackberry and sugar mixture to a simmer over medium heat and cook for 30 to 45 minutes, until reduced by half or the mixture reaches jam thickness. Gently stir.

STRAWBERRY PRESERVES

- 4 cups strawberries (fresh or frozen)
- 1 cup sugar

Place strawberries in colander, rinse with cold water, and drain. Trim tops of berries if needed and cut in half.

Place strawberries in a large pot with sugar. Let sit for 2 hours or until the berries release their juices.

Bring strawberries and sugar mixture to a simmer over medium heat. Cook for 30 to 45 minutes, stirring occasionally until reduced by half or mixture reaches jam thickness.

PEACH PRESERVES

- 2 (16-ounce) cans peaches in syrup
- 2 cups sugar

In a large pot over low heat, cook the peaches with their syrup, stirring occasionally, for 30 to 45 minutes. Do not over-stir or the fruit will break down.

Add sugar, increase heat to medium, and continue to cook until mixture is reduced by three-quarters or reaches jam thickness (about 10 to 12 minutes).

Note: Jar the preserves straight from the pot, filling each jar to the top. Seal as tightly as possible.

DRESSINGS & SPREADS

Pimento Cheese

SERVES 6

Around our neck of the woods, Pimento Cheese is so beloved that it's often referred to as the "pâté of the South." Perfect for party dips or sandwich spreads, this Southern staple is an easy, can't-miss dip that will please any crowd. We recommend topping the Pimento Cheese with sliced scallions and crumbled bacon before serving.

- ½ cup canned pimento peppers, rinsed, drained, and diced
- 2 cups sharp cheddar cheese, shredded
- ⅔ cup mayonnaise
- 1 teaspoon Worcestershire sauce
- ¼ teaspoon garlic powder
- ¼ teaspoon white pepper
- ½ teaspoon salt
- 1 box of your favorite crackers or baguette slices

In a medium bowl, mix all ingredients until fully combined. Refrigerate for at least 1 hour before serving with crackers or baguette slices.

Note: It's important to rinse and drain the pimento peppers to maintain the color and flavor of your cheese spread.

DRESSINGS & SPREADS

Cranberry Bourbon Relish

SERVES 15

A little more piquant and a tad tipsier than your typical Cranberry Relish (thanks to the orange zest and bourbon), this tangy rendition of the holiday classic will take a prominent seat at your Thanksgiving table.

Preheat oven to 325 degrees.

Zest orange, then slice and set aside.

In a 2-inch deep casserole dish, place cranberries. Evenly sprinkle orange zest, cinnamon, and sugar over the berries. Cover with orange slices and foil then bake for 30 to 45 minutes. When berries are tender, remove from oven and pour bourbon over the relish. Squeeze juice from orange slices then discard.

Cover relish with foil, return to oven, and cook for an additional 30 minutes.

Remove relish from oven and stir thoroughly. Cool to room temperature, place in airtight container, and refrigerate until completely cooled (or overnight).

- 1 orange
- 2 pounds frozen whole cranberries, thawed
- 2 teaspoons cinnamon
- 1½ cups sugar
- 1 tablespoon bourbon

Blue Cheese Dressing

MAKES 4 CUPS

- 1 cup crumbled blue cheese, divided
- 1 cup milk
- 2 cups mayonnaise
- ¼ teaspoon Lawry's® Seasoned Salt
- ¼ teaspoon granulated garlic
- 1 teaspoon Worcestershire sauce
- ½ teaspoon lemon juice

From chicken wings to wedge salads, this Blue Cheese Dressing is a winner on just about everything. Pro tip: throw a spoonful of the dressing on a piping hot baked potato and thank us later.

In a medium bowl, whisk together ½ cup crumbled blue cheese and the remaining ingredients until well-blended.

Gently stir in remaining blue cheese. Store in a sealed glass container and refrigerate until ready to serve.

Honey Mustard

MAKES 2½ CUPS

- 2 cups mayonnaise
- 1 teaspoon paprika
- ½ cup honey
- 6 tablespoons yellow mustard
- ½ teaspoon lemon juice

Your chicken tender's new best friend, this classic dipper can also double as a delicious salad dressing or sandwich spread.

In a medium bowl, whisk together all ingredients. Store in a sealed glass container and refrigerate until ready to serve.

DRESSINGS & SPREADS

Peach Vinaigrette

MAKES 3 CUPS

We take great pride in making all of our Loveless Cafe dressings in-house. Our favorite way to use this Peach Vinaigrette is on a salad with some spiced pecans thrown in for a little extra crunch and flavor.

Chop peaches into large chunks. Combine chopped peaches, vinegar, honey, and orange juice concentrate in a blender. Blend until completely smooth. While blender is running, slowly add oil to emulsify.

Add salt and pepper. Store in a sealed glass container and refrigerate until ready to serve.

- 4 medium ripe peaches, peeled and pitted (or 1¼ pound frozen peach slices)
- ½ cup apple cider vinegar
- ⅓ cup honey
- ¼ cup orange juice concentrate
- 1½ cups canola oil
- Salt (to taste)
- Ground black pepper (to taste)

Thousand Island Dressing

MAKES 1½ CUPS

This versatile dressing is named after the Thousand Islands region of upstate New York where it was first used as a condiment in the early 20th century. It can easily be whipped together from refrigerator staples and goes great on salads, burgers, and sandwiches.

In a small bowl, mix all ingredients until well-blended. Store in a sealed glass container and refrigerate until ready to serve.

- 1 cup mayonnaise
- 2 tablespoons chili sauce
- ¼ cup sweet relish
- 1 teaspoon lemon juice
- 1 teaspoon Worcestershire sauce
- 2 tablespoons ketchup

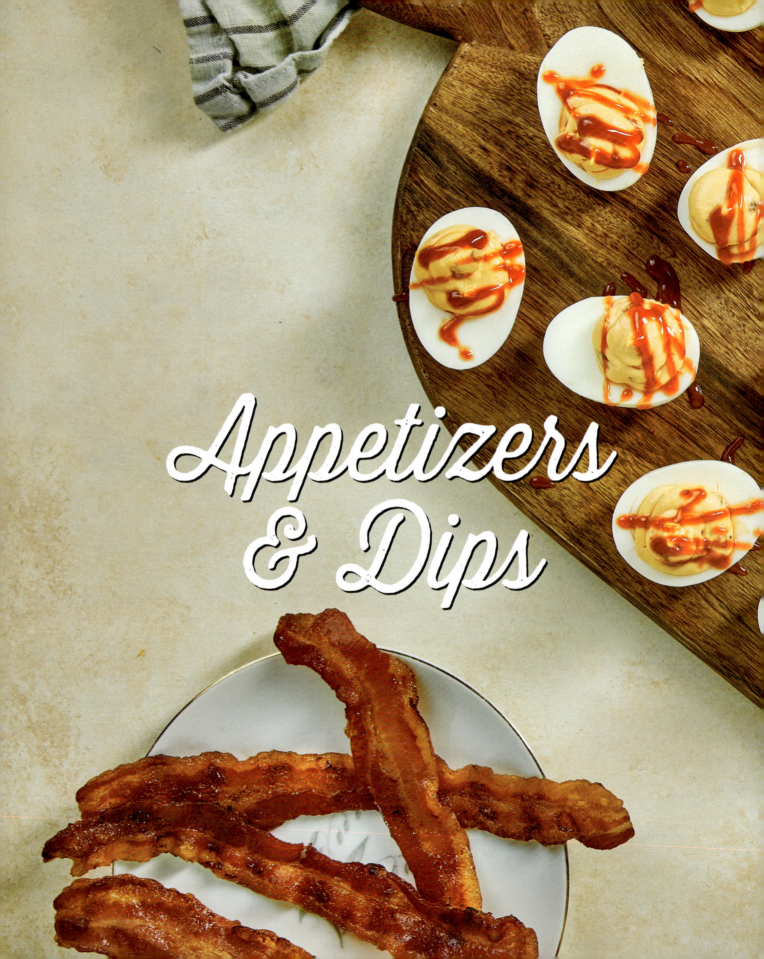

Appetizers & Dips

APPETIZERS & DIPS

Mac n' Bacon Jalapeños

MAKES 16

Say hello to the new MVP of your gameday tailgate! These easy-to-make bacon-wrapped jalapeños are stuffed with our classic Heat n' Eat Macaroni and Cheese and are sure to score a touchdown with your friends and family.

- ½ pan Loveless Cafe Heat n' Eat Macaroni and Cheese (or make your own, recipe on page 107)
- 8 fresh jalapeño peppers
- Cooking oil
- ¼ cup cheddar cheese, shredded
- ½ pound Loveless Cafe Applewood Smoked Country Bacon, uncooked*

Cook macaroni and cheese according to package instructions. Set aside and allow to cool.

Preheat oven to 400 degrees.

Slice each pepper in half lengthwise, removing seeds and any white fleshy parts. Place peppers on a baking sheet that has been sprayed with cooking oil. Stuff each pepper with macaroni and cheese using a small spoon.

Top peppers with shredded cheese. Cut each slice of bacon in half (horizontally) and wrap stuffed peppers in bacon. Bake for 15 to 20 minutes or until peppers are roasted and bacon is crisp.

*Note: If you prefer, you can cook the bacon separately, then cool, chop, and sprinkle on top of peppers when they come out of the oven.

APPETIZERS & DIPS

Blackberry Bruschetta

MAKES APPROXIMATELY 20 PIECES

From weddings and birthday parties to fundraisers and family reunions, we host all kinds of events in the Loveless Barn. No matter the style or size of the shindig, our Blackberry Bruschetta is always the belle of the ball. It's a tangy twist on traditional bruschetta and one of the most popular passed appetizers we serve.

Cut bread into ½-inch thick slices. In a small bowl, mix olive oil and granulated garlic. Lightly drizzle or use a brush to spread oil mixture onto one side of each bread slice, evenly coating the entire side.

Grill or sauté the bread on medium-high heat, oil side down first. Heat for 3 to 5 minutes per side until the bread is crisp on top and bottom, but still soft on the inside. Remove bread slices from pan and place on tray.

To assemble, spread ½ tablespoon Blackberry Preserves on the oiled side of the bread slices. Top with 1 teaspoon chopped Spiced Pecans and 1 teaspoon Gorgonzola crumbles, then serve.

- 1 (11-inch) loaf Cuban bread or soft baguette
- 4 tablespoons olive oil
- ½ teaspoon granulated garlic
- ¾ cup Loveless Cafe Blackberry Preserves
- 4 ounces Loveless Cafe Spiced Pecans, chopped into ¼-inch pieces*
- 4 ounces crumbled Gorgonzola cheese

*For a delicious substitute, try Loveless Cafe Piggy Pecans (made with real bits of bacon) instead of Spiced Pecans.

APPETIZERS & DIPS

Calico Corn Relish Dip

SERVES 6 TO 8

No trip to the Cafe is complete without stopping by Hams & Jams Country Market for a jar of our Loveless Cafe Corn Relish. We recommend combining it with some of our Loveless Cafe Chicken Shake and Loveless Cafe Plain Ol' Hot Sauce to create a highly addictive appetizer that is ideal for entertaining.

- 1 jar Loveless Cafe Corn Relish, drained well
- ¼ cup plus 1 tablespoon sour cream
- ½ tablespoon Loveless Cafe Chicken Shake
- 1 to 2 drops Loveless Cafe Plain Ol' Hot Sauce (optional)
- 1 box of your favorite crackers or chips

Add drained Corn Relish, sour cream, Chicken Shake, and Hot Sauce to a medium bowl. Stir until thoroughly mixed.

Refrigerate for at least 1 hour or overnight. Serve with crackers or chips.

APPETIZERS & DIPS

Zesty Peach and Cream Cheese Dip

SERVES 6

Keep stress and cleanup to a minimum with this slightly spicy appetizer that is simple to prepare, but always makes a statement. We recommend keeping the pantry stocked with these four ingredients so you're always prepared for last minute guests.

- ¾ cup Loveless Cafe Peach Preserves
- 2 tablespoons prepared horseradish
- 1 (8-ounce) block cream cheese
- 1 box of your favorite crackers

In a small mixing bowl, combine Peach Preserves with horseradish. Mix well and set aside.

Place cream cheese block on a medium-sized plate. Pour preserves mixture evenly over the cream cheese.

Serve with your favorite crackers.

APPETIZERS & DIPS

BBQ Bacon Deviled Eggs

SERVES 12

This Southern-inspired twist on a classic appetizer celebrates the love affair of bacon and eggs, with a dash of Loveless Cafe Sweet with a Bite BBQ Sauce mixed in for good measure.

Remove egg yolks from egg whites, reserving yolks. Rinse egg whites and carefully pat dry.

In a mixing bowl, combine yolks, bacon, BBQ Sauce, Worcestershire sauce, and 2 tablespoons mayonnaise. If mixture is too thick, add an extra tablespoon of mayonnaise.

Fill each egg white with a dollop of the yolk mixture. Garnish tops with BBQ Sauce.

Refrigerate until ready to serve.

- 12 hard-boiled eggs (chilled and cut in half lengthwise)
- 6 slices Loveless Cafe Hickory Smoked Pepper Bacon, cooked and chopped
- 1 tablespoon Loveless Cafe Sweet with a Bite BBQ Sauce (plus extra for garnish)
- 1 teaspoon Worcestershire sauce
- 2 to 3 tablespoons mayonnaise

APPETIZERS & DIPS

Chow Chow Deviled Eggs

SERVES 12

Chow Chow is a true Tennessee treat that goes great on beans, chili, and soups. But one of our all-time favorite ways to use the Southern sweet and sour relish is in deviled eggs, which gives them a little more zest than the traditional style.

- 12 hard-boiled eggs (chilled and cut in half lengthwise)
- 1 cup Loveless Cafe Mild Chow Chow, drained and chopped (use Hot Chow Chow for a spicier version)
- 1 teaspoon prepared horseradish
- ¼ cup mayonnaise
- Salt (to taste)
- Ground black pepper (to taste)
- Smoked chili seasoning (optional)
- Fresh parsley, chopped (optional)

Remove egg yolks from egg whites, reserving yolks. Rinse egg whites and carefully pat dry.

In a mixing bowl, combine yolks, Chow Chow, horseradish, and mayonnaise. Add salt and pepper.

Fill each egg white with a spoonful of the prepared filling. Garnish tops with a sprinkle of smoked chili seasoning and chopped parsley, if desired. Refrigerate until ready to serve.

APPETIZERS & DIPS

Hot Pepper Relish Dip

SERVES 4 TO 6

- 1 (8-ounce) container whipped cream cheese
- 1 tablespoon sugar
- 1 jar Loveless Cafe Hot Pepper Relish, drained well
- 1 box of your favorite crackers

Our old-fashioned Hot Pepper Relish is excellent on anything from hot dogs to pizza, but it's much more than a mere condiment. When mixed with cream cheese, it creates an appetizer that's sure to spice up any party. If you're not a fan of spicy food, try making this dip with Loveless Cafe Sweet Pepper Relish.

Place cream cheese and sugar in a medium-sized mixing bowl. Add Hot Pepper Relish and mix well until combined.

Refrigerate for 1 hour. Serve with your favorite crackers.

Sweet Red Pepper Cream Cheese Bites

MAKES ABOUT 8 DOZEN

- 2 (8-ounce) containers whipped cream cheese
- 1 box of your favorite crackers
- 1 jar Loveless Cafe Sweet Pepper Relish, drained well

Another great option for gameday gatherings, this tangy appetizer is easy to assemble and a proven crowd-pleaser.

Spread 1 teaspoon cream cheese onto each cracker. Top with 1 teaspoon Sweet Pepper Relish. Refrigerate until ready to serve.

Creamy Strawberry Preserves Dip

MAKES 3 CUPS

A can't-miss hit for bridal and baby showers or any special occasion, this dip whips together in mere minutes. We recommend serving it with graham crackers or fresh fruit.

In a medium bowl, mix whipped cream cheese and Strawberry Preserves together until blended. Fold in whipped topping, marshmallow creme, and lemon zest. Cover and refrigerate until ready to serve.

- 1 (8-ounce) container whipped cream cheese
- ½ cup Loveless Cafe Strawberry Preserves
- 1 cup whipped topping
- 1 cup marshmallow creme
- Zest of 1 lemon

APPETIZERS & DIPS

BBQ Stuffed Corn Muffins

MAKES 24 MUFFINS

Packed with pulled pork and cheddar cheese, these meal-worthy muffins make great sides and starters. They're also the perfect way to use leftover pulled pork, on the off chance there is some in the fridge.

- 2 eggs
- 3 cups milk
- 2½ cups yellow cornmeal
- 2 cups all-purpose flour
- ⅔ teaspoon salt
- 1 teaspoon ground black pepper
- ½ cup sugar
- 2½ tablespoons baking powder
- 3 tablespoons Loveless Cafe Peach-B-Q Rub, divided
- 4 tablespoons parsley, minced
- ⅔ cup green onion, thinly sliced
- ⅔ cup cheddar cheese
- Non-stick baking spray
- 1 pound pulled pork
- 1 cup Loveless Cafe Sweet with a Bite BBQ Sauce

Preheat oven to 325 degrees.

In a large bowl, combine eggs and milk. In a separate mixing bowl, combine cornmeal, flour, salt, pepper, sugar, baking powder, and 2 tablespoons Peach-B-Q Rub.

Combine both bowls and mix well, then add parsley, green onion, and cheddar cheese.

Coat inside of a mini muffin tin with non-stick spray and line all 24 tins with flour. Scoop 3 ounces of batter into each muffin tin.

Roll pulled pork into ½-ounce balls and place in middle of batter. Top with a pinch of remaining Peach-B-Q Rub and bake for 15 to 17 minutes, until golden brown on top.

Top each muffin with BBQ Sauce or serve sauce on the side.

Supper

SUPPER

Famous Fried Chicken

SERVES 4

Ever since 1951, we've been cooking our Famous Fried Chicken using the original recipe from Annie Loveless. And yes, we'll be keeping it under lock and key right alongside our biscuit recipe. However, with our Loveless Cafe Fried Chicken Breading and this recipe, you can replicate the famously crispy Fried Chicken we've been serving for decades at home.

- 1 fryer chicken (3 pounds or less)
- 3 tablespoons salt
- 2 cups Loveless Cafe Fried Chicken Breading
- Vegetable oil (for frying)

Cut chicken into eight pieces and rinse. Soak in cold salted water for 30 minutes. Drain and pat dry.

Pour Fried Chicken Breading into a bowl. Heat 1 inch of vegetable oil in a large skillet over medium-high heat (375 degrees in an electric skillet).

Dredge chicken in breading, coating well on all surfaces. Pat off excess breading and place chicken in hot oil, making sure pieces are not touching each other.

When chicken is browned (approximately 5 minutes), turn pieces over and reduce heat to medium (300 degrees). Cover and cook for 20 minutes.

Remove lid, increase heat to medium-high and flip chicken. Cook an additional 5 to 7 minutes, until crispy and golden brown.

Drain chicken on a paper towel before serving.

SUPPER

Nashville Hot Chicken

SERVES 4

This just might be the most Music City meal ever! Start with Loveless Cafe's Famous Fried Chicken, then toss it in our signature spicy sauce to make a truly authentic version of the iconic Nashville Hot Chicken.

MAKE NASHVILLE HOT SAUCE

Combine spices in a large mixing bowl. Add melted butter and mix well. Add Hot Sauce and mix until color is consistent.

MAKE FRIED CHICKEN

Cut chicken into eight pieces and rinse. Soak in cold, salted water for 30 minutes. Drain and pat dry.

Pour Fried Chicken Breading into a bowl. Heat 1 inch of vegetable oil in a large skillet over medium-high heat (375 degrees in an electric skillet).

Dredge chicken in breading, coating well on all surfaces. Pat off excess breading and place chicken in hot oil, making sure pieces are not touching each other.

When chicken is browned (approximately 5 minutes), turn pieces over and reduce heat to medium (300 degrees). Cover and cook for 20 minutes.

Remove lid, increase heat to medium-high and flip chicken. Cook an additional 5 to 7 minutes.

Remove chicken from skillet, drain on a paper towel, then toss with Nashville Hot Sauce. Serve on sliced bread topped with dill pickle chips and sprinkled with kosher salt.

NASHVILLE HOT SAUCE

- ¼ cup plus 1 tablespoon cayenne pepper
- ⅛ cup granulated garlic
- 1 teaspoon paprika
- 1 teaspoon salt
- 2 cups unsalted butter, melted
- ¼ cup Loveless Cafe Plain Ol' Hot Sauce

FRIED CHICKEN

- 1 fryer chicken (3 pounds or less)
- 3 tablespoons salt
- 2 cups Loveless Cafe Fried Chicken Breading
- Vegetable oil (for frying)
- 8 slices Texas toast (or thick-cut white bread)
- Dill pickle chips (optional)
- ½ teaspoon kosher salt

Honey Fire Chicken

SERVES 10

CHICKEN AND BRINE

- 5 whole chickens, cut in half
- 2½ quarts water
- 1 (9-ounce) can chipotle peppers
- 4 cups apple cider vinegar
- 1⅓ cups chicken broth
- 7 garlic cloves
- ½ onion, sliced
- 3 teaspoons cayenne pepper
- 1¾ cups sugar
- ½ cup kosher salt

SEASONING

- ¾ cup Loveless Cafe Dry Rub
- ¼ cup Poultry Magic® Seasoning
- ¾ cup granulated garlic
- ⅓ cup onion powder
- ⅓ cup paprika
- ¼ cup sugar
- ⅛ cup Lawry's® Seasoned Salt

- 3½ cups honey (for baking glaze)

Feed the whole family with this five-chicken feast or scale back the ingredients for a smaller crowd. Either way, plan ahead because this recipe calls for the birds to take a two-day brine bath before making their way to the smoker.

MAKE BRINE

In a large container, mix all brine ingredients together then add chicken halves. Cover and refrigerate for 2 days.

MAKE SEASONING

Combine all seasoning mix ingredients together. Blend well and store in an airtight container.

MAKE CHICKEN

Preheat smoker to 225 degrees. Remove chicken from brine, pat dry, and cover all over with seasoning.

Place seasoned chicken skin side down in smoker for 1 hour. Flip and smoke until internal temperature reaches 140 degrees. Remove chicken from smoker.

Preheat oven to 350 degrees.

Heat honey in a double boiler then pour over chicken halves. Place on greased baking sheet and bake for 30 minutes or until chicken reaches an internal temperature of 165 degrees.

Grilled Drunken Pork Loin

SERVES 8

This intoxicatingly delicious pork bathes in an orange juice brine for 24 hours before it's finished with a whiskey wash. It's also spiked with our signature Dry Rub and Peach Preserves, making it an instant classic for summertime cookouts.

MAKE BRINE

Mix all ingredients except ice together in a large stock pot. Over medium-high heat, bring brine to a boil for 5 minutes. Remove from stovetop and place in a container large enough for brine and pork loin then add ice. Once brine has completely cooled, place pork loin in liquid and marinate for 24 hours in the refrigerator.

MAKE PORK

Preheat grill to 400 degrees and oven to 325 degrees.

Remove pork loin from brine, then pat dry and season all over with rubs. Place pork loin on heated grill and char long enough for grill marks to appear on both sides.

Place pork loin on a large baking sheet, then bake for 30 to 45 minutes until internal temperature reaches at least 145 degrees. Allow pork loin to rest for 10 minutes before slicing.

MAKE GLAZE

Mix all ingredients together in a stock pot and heat over medium-low for 15 minutes, stirring occasionally. Drizzle sauce over individual servings of pork.

BRINE

- 4 cups orange juice
- 4 tablespoons salt
- ¼ cup fresh thyme
- 4 tablespoons garlic, chopped
- 4 tablespoons ground black pepper
- 1 bay leaf
- 1 quart ice

PORK

- 1 boneless pork loin (about 3 pounds)
- ¼ cup Loveless Cafe Peach-B-Q Rub
- ¼ cup Loveless Cafe Dry Rub

DRUNKEN PEACH GLAZE

- 3 cups Loveless Cafe Peach Preserves
- 1 cup chicken stock
- 1 tablespoon fresh thyme
- 1 teaspoon salt
- ¼ cup whiskey

SUPPER

Watermelon Ribs

MAKES 2 RACKS OF RIBS

Our pit master arrives at the Loveless Cafe around 4 a.m. most mornings to begin prepping the fire and smoking meats. His hard work never goes unnoticed no matter what he cooks, but it's an extra special treat when he makes Watermelon Ribs. Whenever we run them as a weekly special, guests always remark how it's the first time they've ever tried them. Try making these Southern-style sticky ribs for your next summer cookout. They are sure to be a hit!

- 2 racks St. Louis cut pork spareribs
- 1 bottle Loveless Cafe Dry Rub
- ½ cup brown sugar
- 1 bottle Loveless Cafe Sweet with a Bite BBQ Sauce
- 3 cups watermelon, cut into large cubes

Rub ribs with a blend of the Dry Rub and brown sugar, making sure to cover all surfaces evenly.

Bring smoker to 225 degrees then smoke ribs for 2 hours.

Cut ribs into three bone sections and place in a roasting pan. Cover with BBQ Sauce and watermelon cubes. Wrap pan tightly with foil and braise in oven at 225 degrees for 1½ to 2 hours or until meat is falling off the bone.

SUPPER

Blue Ribbon Salad

SERVES 4

Worthy of a first-place finish, this salad can easily double as a starter or main dish. The veggie chips and Loveless Cafe Spiced Pecans give it a great crunch that pairs to perfection with the peach vinaigrette dressing. To make it a meal, just add chicken or fish.

MAKE VEGETABLE CHIPS

Pour peanut oil into a skillet over medium-high heat. Fry potato and carrot chips until golden brown on both sides (approximately 5 minutes per batch). Drain chips on paper towels and sprinkle with salt.

MAKE SALAD

Divide lettuce among 4 chilled salad plates.

Drizzle peach vinaigrette over salads in a zigzag pattern. Top each plate with 2 tablespoons blue cheese crumbles, 1 tablespoon vegetable chips, and ¼ cup Spiced Pecans.

VEGETABLE CHIPS

- 1 carrot, peeled and shaved lengthwise into thin chips
- 1 russet potato, peeled and shaved lengthwise into thin chips
- ¼ cup peanut oil
- Salt (to taste)

SALAD

- 1 head iceberg lettuce, julienned
- 1 head romaine lettuce, julienned
- 1 cup Peach Vinaigrette (see recipe on page 51)
- ½ cup blue cheese crumbles
- ¼ cup Vegetable Chips
- 1 cup Loveless Cafe Spiced Pecans

Peach Glazed Pork Chops

SERVES 4

The secret to making perfectly moist pork chops is in the brine. Our signature version features juniper berries and Loveless Cafe Peach-B-Q Rub, which gives the pork a pleasantly tart and slightly fruity flavor profile. Make sure you plan ahead though, because you'll want to brine it for at least two days before cooking.

BRINE

- 2 quarts water
- ½ cup salt
- 1 cup orange juice concentrate
- 5 garlic cloves, sliced in half
- 1 cup dark brown sugar
- 6 bay leaves
- 2 tablespoons juniper berries
- 2 tablespoons black peppercorns
- 1 tablespoon mustard seeds
- 2 tablespoons Loveless Cafe Peach-B-Q Rub

PORK LOIN

- 1 boneless pork loin (3 to 4 pounds)
- 2 tablespoons Loveless Cafe Peach-B-Q Rub
- 1 jar Loveless Cafe Peach Preserves

MAKE BRINE

Combine all ingredients in a large container.

Place pork loin into brine so that it is completely submerged. Refrigerate for 2 days.

MAKE PORK LOIN

Remove pork loin from brine and wipe off remaining bits of seasoning.

Liberally coat pork loin with Peach-B-Q Rub.

Bring smoker to 225 degrees. Place pork loin fat side down and smoke for one hour then flip pork loin over, cooking for approximately 45 more minutes. *(Tip: smoke the loin 15 to 20 minutes per pound until it reaches an internal temperature of 135 degrees).*

Approximately 15 minutes before pork loin is done, remove it from smoker and glaze with Peach Preserves.

SUPPER

Place pork loin back in smoker for 15 minutes to allow preserves to thicken. Remove from smoker and cut pork loin into thick chops.

If grill marks are desired, grill over direct heat for 1 minute per side.

Plate pork chops and serve with warm Peach Preserves spooned on top.

SUGGESTIONS AND ALTERNATIVES

If you do not have a smoker, grill the pork loin over direct heat for approximately 4 minutes per side to obtain caramelization and color on the outside of the loin. Grill at 225 degrees for one hour then flip and grill for an additional 45 minutes or until pork loin reaches an internal temperature of 135 degrees. Follow recipe instructions to glaze pork loin and grill for an additional 15 minutes before slicing and serving.

HELPFUL HINTS

Do not let internal temperature of pork loin exceed 150 degrees as it may become dry.

SUPPER

Peach Glazed Country Ham

SERVES 25 TO 35

As delicious as it is decadent, this ham is a stunning centerpiece for any family gathering and can be made on the stovetop or in the oven. The ham can be prepared a day ahead, if desired.

- 1 Loveless Cafe Whole Country Ham
- 1 cup Loveless Cafe Honey, Loveless Cafe Old-Fashioned Sorghum, or brown sugar
- 1½ cups Loveless Cafe Peach Preserves
- 40 to 50 whole cloves
- Fresh fruit and herbs for garnish (optional)

MAKE HAM

Remove any mold* that may be on the surface using a scrub brush. If mold is very heavy, scrape with a knife and rinse ham under warm running water. To reduce saltiness, soak ham in cold water at room temperature for up to 12 hours (optional).

STOVETOP METHOD

Place ham in a large stock pot or Dutch oven. Cut hock off ham if it is too big for pot.

Add enough water to pot to cover ham by about 1-inch. Add Honey, Sorghum, or brown sugar.

Cook over medium-high heat and bring to boil. Reduce heat to low, cover, and simmer for 18 to 20 minutes per pound. Add more water to keep ham covered, if necessary.

Ham is fully cooked when internal temperature reaches 160 degrees.

*Due to aging, your ham will have some mold on it. You may also notice white specks throughout the meat. This in no way affects the quality of the meat but indicates proper aging and is often preferred by many connoisseurs.

OVEN METHOD

Preheat oven to 250 degrees.

Place ham in a large roasting pan on a rack, skin side up. Cut hock off if ham is too big for pan. Add water and Honey, Sorghum, or brown sugar to cover as much of the ham as possible, staying at least 2 inches from top of roaster.

Cover and bake for 18 to 20 minutes per pound. Simmer, do not boil. If water evaporates during cooking process, add more water. *Note: If the water does not cover at least two-thirds of ham, turn ham over halfway through baking time to ensure even cooking.*

Ham is fully cooked when internal temperature reaches 160 degrees.

MAKE GLAZE

Carefully remove ham from water and allow to cool on a baking sheet for 1 hour.

Preheat oven to 400 degrees.

Remove skin with a sharp knife, leaving ¼-inch thick layer of fat. Score ham fat with a sharp knife in a diagonal pattern. Repeat scoring diagonally in opposite direction to create a crossing pattern. Spread with Peach Preserves and insert whole cloves at crossings.

Bake until glaze is bubbly and brown, approximately 10 to 15 minutes. Do not overcook.

Cool slightly and transfer ham to a serving platter. Garnish platter with fresh cut fruit and herbs.

To serve, cut ham into paper thin slices.

STORAGE TIPS

Leave ham in original packaging. Never wrap ham in plastic wrap.

Ham can be hung unrefrigerated in a dry storage room free of pests with good air circulation for as long as you wish to continue aging the ham.

Ham can be frozen for up to one year, which protects against over-aging and pests, and inhibits additional mold formation.

Be careful not to over-age ham at room temperature as it will continue to naturally dry, creating stronger flavor characteristics.

Chicken n' Dumplings

SERVES 4

Just as they're served *at* the Loveless Cafe, with our famous biscuits as the dumplings, of course.

- ½ bag Loveless Cafe Biscuit Mix
- 1⅓ cups buttermilk
- 4 boneless skinless chicken breasts
- 3 quarts chicken stock
- ¼ cup butter
- 1 large onion, julienned
- 1 stalk celery, diced
- ⅛ teaspoon dried thyme
- ⅛ teaspoon dried sage
- Salt (to taste)
- Ground black pepper (to taste)

Prepare Biscuit Mix according to package instructions. Do not roll out dough. Cover dough and refrigerate until needed.

In a large stock pot over medium-high heat, boil chicken breasts in chicken stock until fully cooked (approximately 10 minutes). Remove chicken from pot, let cool, then cut into quarter-sized pieces and set aside, keeping the stock hot until needed.

In a large skillet, melt butter over medium heat then sauté onion and celery until translucent. Add sautéed onions and celery to hot chicken stock. Stir in thyme, sage, salt, and pepper. Bring to a boil then reduce to a simmer.

Scoop out dough using two small spoons to create dollops that are approximately the size of a nickel. Add a batch of 12 to 15 dumplings at a time to stock pot. Allow to simmer for approximately 5 minutes before adding another batch. Repeat with remaining dumplings.

After simmering for 1 hour, add chopped chicken and simmer for 15 to 20 minutes more. Check for seasoning and adjust with salt and pepper to taste.

Fried Catfish

SERVES 8

The secret to our special recipe for fish fry Fridays? Using both cornmeal and all-purpose flour for the breading. It's not just delicious on catfish either. Try it out on any fish fry. We even use it for our fried green tomatoes.

Combine cornmeal, 2 cups all-purpose flour, black pepper, dry mustard, and lemon pepper in a large mixing bowl. Pour mixture into a shallow pie plate or baking dish then pour ½ cup flour into a separate shallow dish.

Preheat oil in a large skillet over medium-high heat.

Dredge catfish fillets in flour then press cornmeal mixture into the catfish on both sides. Working in batches, place catfish in hot skillet and fry on both sides until golden brown (approximately 5 minutes per side). Drain on paper towels before serving.

- 1½ cups yellow cornmeal
- 2½ cups all-purpose flour, divided
- 1 tablespoon ground black pepper
- 1 tablespoon dry mustard
- 1 tablespoon lemon pepper
- Canola oil (for frying)
- 8 catfish fillets

SUPPER

Blackberry BBQ Chicken Halves

MAKES 4 CHICKEN HALVES

Blackberry Preserves aren't just for biscuits. They make a great BBQ sauce that helps yield one of the juiciest chickens we've ever tasted. This berry-glazed bird pairs perfectly with creamed corn, macaroni and cheese, and hashbrown casserole. Plan well ahead though, this recipe requires brining the chicken for one to two days before cooking.

BRINE CHICKEN

In a large bowl, mix water, vinegar, bay leaves, garlic, and brown sugar. Set aside.

Split chickens in half, removing backbone. Place chicken in brine and refrigerate for at least 1 day.

Drain chicken and pat dry. Generously sprinkle with Dry Rub.

MAKE CHICKEN

Smoke or grill chicken for approximately 3 hours, or until internal temperature reaches 160 degrees. Remove from heat and coat liberally with BBQ Sauce.

Place on grill or in an oven preheated to 350 degrees for approximately 5 minutes. Be careful not to scorch. Brush with sauce several times while turning chicken until sauce has caramelized and chicken is lightly charred.

- 2 whole chickens
- 3 quarts water
- 2 cups apple cider vinegar
- 6 bay leaves
- 8 garlic cloves, halved
- 1 tablespoon dark brown sugar
- ½ cup Loveless Cafe Dry Rub
- 1 bottle Loveless Cafe Blackberry BBQ Sauce

SUPPER

Smoked Beef Brisket
MAKES 1 BRISKET

Brisket can be one of the trickiest cuts of meat to master. Naturally tough, it requires slow cooking, the right Dry Rub, a good braising liquid, and a whole lot of patience. It's a labor of love performed by our pit master and it has led to countless clean plates in the Cafe.

- 1 beef brisket (10 to 16 pounds)
- 1 cup Loveless Cafe Dry Rub
- 1 gallon water
- 1 quart red wine
- 1 red onion, diced
- 5 garlic cloves, crushed and peeled
- 4 celery sticks, cleaned and cut into 8 pieces
- 1 large carrot, peeled and cut into 8 pieces
- ¼ cup salt
- ¼ cup corn starch

Preheat smoker to 225 degrees.

Unwrap brisket and pat dry. Remove any pieces of fat more than ½-inch thick. Fully season brisket with Dry Rub and let sit for at least 1 hour before cooking.

Place brisket in smoker fat side facing down. Smoke for 3 hours. Flip and smoke for another 4 hours.

In a roasting pan, mix water, red wine, onion, garlic, celery, carrot, and salt. Place the partially smoked brisket into braising liquid. The liquid should cover the meat. Cover top of pan with foil and return to smoker for 10 hours. Check every 2 hours and add more water as needed. *Note: The brisket is finished when the meat is separating when pulling it with a fork, but not quite falling apart.*

Remove brisket from smoker and set aside. Strain braising liquid into a pot and place on stove. Simmer liquid until reduced by at least one-quarter. Thicken with corn starch while simmering, stirring continuously until it reaches the consistency of a loose gravy.

Spoon warm gravy over sliced brisket before serving.

SUPPER

Meatloaf

SERVES 6 TO 8

Always a fan favorite, our meatloaf's magnificent allure comes from the signature Loveless Cafe Dry Rub and Loveless Cafe Sweet with a Bite BBQ Sauce.

Add canola oil to a medium skillet and sauté onion until slightly caramelized. Set aside to cool.

In a large bowl, combine beef, cooled onion, Worcestershire sauce, Dry Rub, salt, black pepper, garlic, half of BBQ Sauce, eggs, and biscuit crumbs. Mix well.

Shape beef mixture into a loaf and place in a 9-by-13 baking dish. Allow to rest for 1 hour before cooking.

Preheat oven to 350 degrees.

Bake covered for 1 hour or until internal temperature reaches 165 degrees.

In a small saucepan, warm the remaining BBQ Sauce and serve on the side.

REHEATING TIPS

Cover with foil and bake at 300 degrees for 45 minutes.

Meatloaf can also be sliced and grilled or pan fried.

- 1 teaspoon canola oil
- ¼ cup onion, diced
- 2½ pounds ground beef
- 2 tablespoons Worcestershire sauce
- 2 tablespoons Loveless Cafe Dry Rub
- ½ tablespoon salt
- ½ tablespoon ground black pepper
- ¼ tablespoon granulated garlic
- 1 bottle Loveless Cafe Sweet with a Bite BBQ Sauce, divided
- 2 eggs
- 1¼ cups biscuit crumbs or bread crumbs

Fried Chicken Cordon Bleu

SERVES 4

There are countless variations of this dish, which traces its origins to Switzerland. Our version offers a Southern twist by stuffing the chicken with Loveless Cafe Country Ham, giving it a richer and more robust flavor.

FRIED CHICKEN

- 4 boneless skinless chicken breasts
- 2 cups all-purpose flour
- 2 cups buttermilk
- 2 cups Loveless Cafe Fried Chicken Breading
- Vegetable oil (for frying)
- 2 slices Swiss cheese, sliced in half to make 4 pieces
- 8 ounces Loveless Cafe Country Ham, cooked and sliced into 4 pieces about 1½-inch long

SAGE CREAM SAUCE

- 2 cups heavy cream
- 1 cup chicken stock
- 1 tablespoon Dijon mustard
- 1 bay leaf
- 1 teaspoon dried sage
- 1 teaspoon salt

MAKE FRIED CHICKEN

Fill fryer with vegetable oil and heat to 300 degrees.

Lay ham on Swiss cheese and roll tight.

Slice a 1-inch hole in the top of chicken breasts and cut halfway down creating a pocket wide enough to be stuffed.

Stuff chicken with rolled ham and Swiss cheese. Close pocket, using toothpicks if necessary.

Pour flour, buttermilk, and Fried Chicken Breading into separate containers large enough for chicken.

Dredge stuffed chicken breasts first with flour, then buttermilk, and lastly in breading.

Fully submerge chicken in vegetable oil and fry for 10 minutes or until golden brown with an internal temperature of 165 degrees.

Pull from fryer and set aside on cooling rack to rest.

MAKE CREAM SAUCE

Pour heavy cream into a saucepan and heat over medium until reduced by one-quarter, stirring occasionally (approximately 5 to 10 minutes). Add chicken stock, mustard, bay leaf, sage, and salt to cream. Simmer over medium heat until sauce has thickened to a smooth gravy consistency.

Remove bay leaf and spoon sauce over chicken breasts.

SUPPER

Smoked Turkey
WITH CRANBERRY BBQ SAUCE

SERVES 4

For far too long, turkey and cranberries have been typecast as a Thanksgiving-only pairing. But if you ask us, the combo is too delicious to enjoy only one day a year. This recipe is great for any occasion or season.

SMOKED TURKEY

- 1 skinless turkey breast (3 to 4 pounds)
- ½ cup Loveless Cafe Chicken Shake
- ½ tablespoon dried thyme

CRANBERRY BBQ SAUCE

- 1 bottle Loveless Cafe Sweet with a Bite BBQ Sauce
- 1 (14-ounce) can whole berry cranberry sauce
- 2 tablespoons lemon juice

MAKE TURKEY

Preheat smoker to 225 degrees.

Fully season turkey with Chicken Shake and dried thyme. Let sit for at least 1 hour before cooking.

Place turkey in smoker and cook for 3 hours. Flip and smoke for 1 hour or until internal temperature reaches 165 degrees. Let turkey rest for 15 minutes before slicing.

MAKE CRANBERRY BBQ SAUCE

In a medium pot, combine BBQ Sauce, cranberry sauce, and lemon juice. Heat over medium-low until the sauce begins to lightly simmer, stirring occasionally. Remove from heat and serve over turkey.

Country Fried Steak

SERVES 4

This classic comfort dish is so popular at the Loveless Cafe that we serve it for breakfast, lunch, and supper. After the steak is finished cooking and removed from the skillet, make sure to save the renderings to make a pan gravy. We highly recommend serving Country Fried Steak with mashed potatoes and lots of gravy. Indeed, it's almost a sin not to here in the South!

Mix garlic, flour, salt, and black pepper in a plastic bag and shake to combine. Pour mixture onto a plate.

Heat oil in a cast iron skillet over medium heat, making sure oil barely covers the bottom of the skillet.

Dredge steaks completely in flour mixture and cook until browned on both sides (approximately 5 minutes per side).

Place cooked steaks on paper towels to drain and pat dry.

- 1 tablespoon granulated garlic
- ½ cup all-purpose flour
- 2 tablespoons salt
- 1 tablespoon ground black pepper
- Canola oil (for frying)
- 4 steak cutlets or cube steaks, tenderized

SUPPER

Blackened Peach BBQ Salmon
WITH TOMATO SALAD
SERVES 4

BLACKENED PEACH BBQ SALMON

- 4 skinless salmon filets
- 2 tablespoons Loveless Cafe Peach-B-Q Rub
- 2 tablespoons blackened seasoning

TOMATO SALAD

- 1 cup diced tomato
- 1 tablespoon parsley, diced
- 1 tablespoon chives, diced
- 1 teaspoon kosher salt
- ½ teaspoon cracked black pepper
- ½ teaspoon garlic powder
- 1 tablespoon olive oil

One of the many delicious ways to use our versatile Loveless Cafe Peach-B-Q Rub is on seafood. Meaty fish such as salmon are great for grilling, and its rich flavor blends brilliantly with the rub's all-natural herbs and spices.

MAKE SALMON

Mix Peach-B-Q Rub and blackened seasoning in small bowl. Pat salmon dry with paper towels. Apply seasoning on both sides of salmon. Cook in a sauté pan or over an open flame grill until it reaches desired doneness.

MAKE TOMATO SALAD

Mix tomatoes, parsley, chives, salt, pepper, garlic powder, and olive oil in a bowl. Refrigerate at least 20 minutes before serving.

TO SERVE

Plate salmon and spoon tomato salad on top.

SUPPER

Blackberry Scallops

MAKES 6 SCALLOPS

It's not all chicken and biscuits here at the Loveless Cafe. We're big fans of seafood too, especially scallops smothered in our signature Blackberry Preserves.

MAKE SCALLOPS

Dry scallops completely using a paper towel then cover tops and bottoms with Cajun seasoning.

Heat a 12-inch sauté pan over medium-high. Melt butter until it foams and turns lightly brown, being careful not to scorch.

Place scallops flat side down in melted butter and cook for 1 to 3 minutes. Flip when the bottom is seared and the seasoning has created a light crust. Cook the other side to the same sear. *Note: Be careful not to overcook scallops. The inside should change from a milky translucent appearance to white with a firmer texture.*

Set scallops aside while making sauce.

MAKE BLACKBERRY SAUCE

Reduce heat on sauté pan to medium. Add butter and let melt. Add shallots and bay leaf then sauté until they are light brown. Add white wine to deglaze pan and cook for 30 seconds then remove bay leaf. Add Blackberry Preserves. Lightly stir until sauce is hot and begins to bubble. Remove from heat then add salt and pepper.

PLATING

Place scallops on serving plate. Top each scallop with 2 tablespoons of sauce. Garnish with chives, green onion, or parsley.

SCALLOPS

- 6 raw sea scallops (U-10 preferred)
- 1 teaspoon Cajun seasoning
- 2 tablespoons unsalted butter

BLACKBERRY SAUCE

- 1 tablespoon unsalted butter
- 3 tablespoons shallots, julienned
- 1 bay leaf
- 3 tablespoons dry white wine
- ½ cup Loveless Cafe Blackberry Preserves
- Salt and pepper (to taste)
- 2 tablespoons chives, green onions, or parsley, chopped (optional)

Sides

SIDES

Creamed Corn

SERVES 10

This dish always earns rave reviews from our guests. Now you can enjoy it in the comfort of your own home!

Divide corn into two pots: 4 cups into one pot and 6 cups into a second pot.

To the 4-cup pot, add 3 cups water, ½ cup sugar, and 1 tablespoon kosher salt. Add remaining water, sugar, and kosher salt to the 6-cup pot.

Place both pots on stove and bring to a boil then immediately remove from heat.

Drain the 6-cup pot of corn in a colander then return drained corn to the pot. Add ¼ cup butter and set aside.

Drain the 4-cup pot of corn in a colander then return drained corn to the pot. Add ¼ cup butter and heavy cream. Return pot to stove, bring to a boil, then remove from heat.

Purée cream and corn mixture in a blender or food processor until smooth. Add the puréed mixture to the whole corn and mix thoroughly. Season with salt and pepper.

TIMESAVING TIP

If you're short on time, our Heat n' Eat Creamed Corn is always available on our website for homemade Southern cooking without the fuss.

- 10 cups sweet corn kernels (fresh or frozen), divided
- 6 cups water, divided
- 2 cups sugar, divided
- 4 tablespoons kosher salt, divided
- ½ cup unsalted butter, divided
- 1 cup heavy cream
- Salt (to taste)
- Ground black pepper (to taste)

SIDES

Cucumbers & Onions

SERVES 8

This simple and splendid summer salad is best enjoyed with peak season cucumbers (from May through August). It's the perfect accompaniment to grilled meats like BBQ chicken and ribs.

- 1 cup apple cider vinegar
- ½ cup sugar
- 3 large cucumbers, peeled and cut into ½-inch rounds
- 1 small yellow onion, peeled and cut into thin slices
- 1 teaspoon salt
- 1 teaspoon pepper
- Dash of fresh lemon juice

Pour vinegar and sugar into a small pot, then cook over medium heat for 4 to 6 minutes, melting the sugar without boiling the vinegar. Remove from heat and let cool.

Combine cucumbers and onions in a large serving bowl. Pour the cooled vinegar mixture over the cucumbers and onions, stirring gently to combine. Add salt, pepper, and lemon juice.

Refrigerate for at least 1 hour and serve chilled.

SIDES

Brown Sugar Glazed Carrots

SERVES 4 TO 6

These sliced carrots are simple enough to whip together for a quick weeknight side, but delicious enough to earn a coveted spot at the holiday dinner table. Created by our talented Loveless Events culinary team, they've become a fixture at shindigs of all styles in the Loveless Barn.

- 2 quarts water
- 2 pounds whole carrots, peeled and sliced into ½-inch diagonals
- 2 tablespoons butter
- 1 cup brown sugar, packed
- ¾ tablespoon salt
- Fresh parsley or mint for garnish, chopped (optional)

In a large pot, bring water to boil. Place carrots in colander, lower colander into water, and blanch for 3 minutes. Remove colander and drain carrots.

Heat skillet over medium and add butter. When butter is melted, add carrots and sauté until they begin to brown (approximately 5 minutes).

Add brown sugar and salt then turn heat to low, being careful not to burn the sugar. Stir until carrots are coated, making sure sugar is not sticking to the bottom of the pan. Stir occasionally until carrots are tender.

Pour glazed carrots into a serving bowl. Garnish with fresh chopped parsley or mint and serve hot.

Southern Macaroni and Cheese

SERVES 16

Everyone's favorite side, our Southern Macaroni and Cheese is decadent enough to double as a standalone supper. Now you can recreate the same recipe that we've been serving for decades at the Loveless Cafe. Don't worry—if you want to tell your friends that you came up with the recipe on your own, we're fine with that too.

Preheat oven to 375 degrees.

Grease a large rectangular baking dish and set aside.

Bring water and ½ tablespoon salt to boil in a stock pot. Add macaroni, stirring occasionally. For creamy Macaroni and Cheese, be sure to cook the pasta until limp, not al dente (approximately 7 to 8 minutes). Drain macaroni and pour into the prepared baking dish.

In a heavy saucepan, melt butter over medium heat. Add flour and stir until very lightly browned to make a roux then remove from heat. Heat milk in a separate pan over medium heat and whisk into the roux. Bring to a low boil to thicken then add remaining salt, cayenne, and cheeses. Remove from heat and stir well until cheese is melted.

Pour cheese mixture over the cooked macaroni and mix well. Bake for 10 to 15 minutes then serve.

2	quarts water
1½	tablespoons salt
2	pounds elbow macaroni, uncooked
½	cup unsalted butter
¾	cup all-purpose flour
½	gallon milk
½	teaspoon cayenne pepper
½	cup blue cheese crumbles
4	cups cheddar cheese, shredded
1	pound pasteurized soft American cheese (such as Velveeta®)

TIMESAVING TIP

If you're in a rush, our Heat n' Macaroni and Cheese is easy, cheesy, breezy, and always available on our website for homemade Southern cooking without the fuss.

SIDES

Southern Turnip Greens

SERVES 8 TO 10

- 1 tablespoon canola oil
- 4 ounces Loveless Cafe Applewood Smoked Country Bacon, roughly chopped
- 1 medium onion, chopped
- ½ pound Loveless Cafe Country Ham, finely chopped
- 1 teaspoon crushed red pepper
- ¼ cup Loveless Cafe Honey
- ⅔ cup apple cider vinegar
- 1 quart water (plus more as needed)
- 4 pounds turnip greens, washed, trimmed, and roughly chopped
- Salt (to taste)
- Ground black pepper (to taste)

While we use this technique for Turnip Greens at the Cafe, this recipe will work beautifully for collards, mustards, kale, or any other greens you might have on hand. Because greens can vary in bitterness with the season, this is a dish you'll want to taste occasionally as you cook and adjust seasonings accordingly.

Add canola oil to a large stock pot over low heat. Cook bacon until fat is rendered, stirring occasionally (approximately 5 minutes).

Add onion, increase heat to medium, and cook until onions are translucent. Add ham, red pepper, Honey, vinegar, and water, bringing to a boil.

Add greens, stirring until they boil down. Simmer for about 4 hours, adding more water as necessary so greens are covered in pot. Once greens are tender, season with salt and pepper.

Note: The juice from cooking turnip greens is called "pot liquor" and can be used for dipping your biscuits or cornbread.

SIDES

Bacon Balsamic Glazed Brussels Sprouts

SERVES 4 TO 6

Everything tastes better with bacon, right? Especially when it's made with our signature Loveless Cafe Applewood Smoked Country Bacon. Created by our Loveless Events team, these sautéed Brussels Sprouts make a quick and easy side dish that is packed with flavor.

- 2 pounds fresh Brussels sprouts, washed, trimmed, and cut in half
- 2 tablespoons butter
- ¼ cup Loveless Cafe Applewood Smoked Country Bacon, cooked and chopped
- 1 tablespoon salt
- ½ cup chicken stock
- 3 tablespoons balsamic vinegar, divided

Fill medium stock pot about three-quarters full with water and bring to a boil. Add brussels sprouts to boiling water and blanch for 1 to 2 minutes. Be careful not to overcook.

Drain Brussels sprouts in a colander. Melt butter in a medium skillet over medium heat, stirring occasionally. Add Brussels sprouts and cook until the sprouts turn golden brown (approximately 6 to 8 minutes).

Add in cooked bacon, sprinkle with salt, and cook for another 2 minutes. Add chicken stock and cook for 2 minutes then stir in 2 tablespoons balsamic vinegar.

Remove from heat, pour into a serving dish, and drizzle with remaining balsamic vinegar.

SIDES

Black-Eyed Peas

SERVES 4

These Southern-style Black-Eyed Peas, also known as Hoppin' John, are believed to bring good luck and prosperity to those who eat them on New Year's Day. We like to serve them with our Loveless Cafe Chow Chow and frankly, would be very happy eating them all year long.

- 1 pound fresh or dried black-eyed peas (presoak dry beans according to package instructions)
- 1 quart water
- ½ pound smoked ham hock
- 1 teaspoon garlic salt
- Ground black pepper (to taste)
- 1 tablespoon crushed red pepper
- Loveless Cafe Chow Chow (for garnish)

Combine peas and water in a large pot. Add ham hock, garlic salt, black pepper, and red pepper.

Bring to a boil then reduce heat and let simmer 1 hour or until the peas are tender. Stir occasionally, adding water if needed.

Remove ham hock, cut meat from bone, then stir ham pieces into cooked peas. Serve with a topping of Chow Chow.

Caramel Sweet Potatoes

SERVES 6 TO 8

A Thanksgiving staple, these sweet potatoes are too good to only eat one day a year. That's why we serve them year-round at the Loveless Cafe. And now you can too!

Preheat oven to 350 degrees. Grease a 9-by-13 baking pan and set aside.

In a large mixing bowl, stir together brown sugar, cinnamon, and orange juice concentrate. Toss sweet potatoes in brown sugar mixture then spread cubes evenly across baking pan.

Top potatoes with pats of butter. Bake uncovered for 1½ to 2 hours until potatoes are tender.

Recipe note: You may substitute equal parts granulated sugar for brown sugar to keep the color of the dish bright.

- 1½ cups brown sugar, lightly packed
- 1 teaspoon cinnamon
- 1 cup orange juice concentrate, thawed
- 6 to 8 medium-sized sweet potatoes, peeled and chopped into large cubes
- ½ cup butter, sliced into pats

SIDES

Fried Green Tomatoes

SERVES 6 TO 8

A tried-and-true Southern staple, Fried Green Tomatoes are one of the most popular sides we serve at the Loveless Cafe. They are quite versatile, too. We recommend adding one to a BLT for some extra pizzazz.

Vegetable oil (enough to fill a large skillet ¼-inch deep)

- 1½ cups buttermilk
- 1½ cups yellow cornmeal
- 2 tablespoons salt
- 2 tablespoons all-purpose flour
- 2 tablespoons ground black pepper
- 1½ teaspoons lemon pepper
- 1 teaspoon dry mustard
- 4 large green tomatoes, sliced ¼-inch to ½-inch thick

Heat oil over medium-high heat in a large skillet.

Pour buttermilk into a shallow dish. In a bowl, mix together cornmeal, salt, flour, pepper, lemon pepper, and dry mustard then pour into a second shallow dish or pie plate. Dip tomato slices into buttermilk then dredge in the cornmeal mixture.

Fry in batches until browned, approximately 3 to 5 minutes on each side.

Enjoy on a BLT, as an appetizer, or as a side dish.

Hush Puppies

SERVES 12

Forever a fish fry favorite, Hush Puppies are a must with the catfish dinners served at the Loveless Cafe. This classic recipe was once featured on the Martha Stewart Show.

Fill a deep skillet with 2 to 3 inches of oil. Heat oil until it reaches 375 degrees on a deep fry thermometer.

In a large bowl, whisk together cornmeal, flour, baking soda, baking powder, and salt. Stir in onions. In a separate bowl, combine egg yolk and buttermilk then stir into cornmeal mixture until combined.

Using an electric mixer fitted with the whisk attachment, beat egg whites until stiff. Gently fold into cornmeal mixture.

Working in batches, drop batter into oil using a 1-ounce scoop and cook, turning once, until the hush puppies rise to the surface and are golden brown (approximately 2 to 3 minutes).

Transfer to a paper towel. Serve immediately.

Canola oil (for frying)
- 2 cups yellow cornmeal
- 2 tablespoons all-purpose flour
- 1 teaspoon baking soda
- 1 teaspoon baking powder
- 1 teaspoon kosher salt
- ½ cup onion, grated
- ¼ cup green onion, thinly sliced
- 1 egg yolk
- 1 cup buttermilk
- 6 egg whites

SIDES

Coleslaw

SERVES 10 TO 12

Slaw is another Southern specialty that we're very fond of here in Tennessee. You can find regional variations of this side dish throughout the country, but we make ours with just the right amount of crunch, creaminess, and tang from the vinegar-spiked dressing. Serve it as a standalone side or smother some pulled pork for a truly blissful barbecue sandwich.

- 2 tablespoons distilled white vinegar
- 2 tablespoons sugar
- 1 teaspoon kosher salt
- 1½ cups mayonnaise
- 2 tablespoons parsley, chopped
- 1 medium head green cabbage, chopped and shredded
- ½ cup red cabbage, shredded
- 2 carrots, grated
- Salt (to taste)
- Ground black pepper (to taste)

Pour vinegar, sugar, and salt into a saucepan. Cook over low heat until sugar dissolves, stirring occasionally.

Remove from heat and pour mixture into a large mixing bowl then allow to cool.

Add mayonnaise and parsley to mixing bowl then stir to combine. Fold in cabbage and carrots. Add salt and pepper.

Refrigerate for at least 1 hour before serving.

Hoe Cakes

SERVES 4

Hoe Cakes are an old-fashioned Southern delicacy that are a cross between cornbread and pancakes. They make a great side dish at any meal, especially ones that involve the Hoe Cakes soaking up delicious sauces.

1½	cups yellow cornmeal
¼	teaspoon baking soda
1¼	cups buttermilk
1	egg, lightly beaten
	Canola oil (for frying)
	Salt (to taste)

Combine cornmeal and baking soda in a mixing bowl. Stir in buttermilk and beaten egg to make batter.

Heat oil in a small skillet over medium-high heat. Pour ½ cup batter into skillet. Fry until golden brown on both sides (approximately 2 to 4 minutes).

Repeat with remaining batter and serve hot.

Grits

SERVES 4

Grits have a religious-like following in the South. Named after the texture of the ground corn used to make the dish, the style and method of cooking grits varies from region to region. We make ours using stone-ground grits and whipping cream for a rich version of the Southern staple that goes great with breakfast, lunch, and dinner.

1	quart water
2	teaspoons salt
2	tablespoons butter
⅔	cup stone-ground grits
⅓	cup heavy cream

Pour water, salt, and butter into a medium pot and bring to a low boil. Pour in grits and stir continuously until grits are soft and fully cooked (approximately 30 minutes). Add cream and mix well to combine. Serve hot.

SIDES

Chow Chow Potato Salad

SERVES 8 TO 10

- 3½ pounds Yukon Gold potatoes, peeled and cut into 1-inch cubes
- 1 tablespoon kosher salt
- 1 cup mayonnaise
- 3 tablespoons spicy brown mustard
- 2 tablespoons apple cider vinegar
- 6 hard-boiled eggs, peeled and chopped
- 3 celery stalks, chopped
- ½ large onion, chopped
- 1 jar Loveless Cafe Mild Chow Chow, drained well
- Salt (to taste)
- Ground black pepper (to taste)
- Paprika (optional garnish)
- Parsley (optional garnish)

Made with our signature Chow Chow, there is nothing bland or boring about this potato salad. A quick and easy side, it has just the right amount of tang and is perfect for picnics.

Place potatoes in a stock pot then cover with cold water and kosher salt. Bring to a boil then reduce to a simmer, cooking about 5 to 10 minutes or until tender. Drain well.

In a medium bowl, combine mayonnaise, mustard, and vinegar. Add potatoes, chopped eggs, celery, onion, and Chow Chow. Toss to combine.

Season with salt and pepper. Garnish with paprika and parsley.

HELPFUL HINTS

Substitute our Hot Chow Chow to spice things up!

Cornbread Dressing

SERVES 12 TO 15

If you grew up in the South, chances are your grandmother had a go-to Cornbread Dressing recipe. The key to a rich, moist dressing is using a homemade or high-quality chicken stock. If the dressing looks a little dry while mixing, add more stock until desired moistness is achieved.

MAKE CORNBREAD

Preheat oven to 400 degrees.

Mix white cornmeal, egg, buttermilk, water, and bacon grease or butter in a bowl. Pour mixture into a greased 9-by-9 baking pan leaving 1 inch at the top for cornbread to rise during cooking.

Cook for 10 minutes then turn baking pan 180 degrees. Cook for an additional 2 to 5 minutes until a toothpick comes out clean. Allow cornbread to cool at room temperature for 1 hour before finishing the dressing.

MAKE DRESSING

Preheat oven to 350 degrees.

Melt butter in a large sauté pan over medium-low heat. Add celery and onion, cooking until translucent. Remove and place in a large mixing bowl then crumble the cornbread in by hand. Add 2 cups chicken stock and begin mixing by hand. Once combined thoroughly, add sage, pepper, salt, and remaining chicken stock. Mix until fully combined.

Pour dressing into a greased 9-by-13 baking dish at least 2 inches deep. Bake for 20 minutes.

Note: For a thicker texture and crispier, golden brown top, continue cooking for an additional 5 to 10 minutes.

CORNBREAD

- 2 cups self-rising white cornmeal
- 1 large egg
- 1 cup buttermilk
- ½ cup water
- ¼ cup bacon grease or melted butter

DRESSING

- ½ cup unsalted butter
- 2 cups celery, diced
- 1 cup white onion, diced
- 2½ cups chicken stock, divided
- 1½ tablespoons dried sage
- ½ tablespoon white pepper
- 1½ tablespoons kosher salt

DRINKS

Hot Cranberry Apple Cider

MAKES ¾ GALLON

A soothing and delicious way to keep warm on winter nights, this hot cider goes from jug to mug in less than 10 minutes.

- ½ gallon apple cider
- 1 jar Loveless Cafe Countrypolitan Moonshine Mixer
- 1 teaspoon pumpkin pie spice
- 1 to 2 cinnamon sticks (optional)

Mix all ingredients in a large pot and bring to a boil then reduce to simmer for 5 minutes.

Pour into coffee mugs and garnish with cinnamon sticks.

DRINKS

Blue Lightnin' Fall Sangria

MAKES 1½ QUARTS

- 1 orange, sliced into wedges
- 1 lemon, sliced into wedges
- 2 cups fresh pineapple, cut into chunks
- 1 green apple, seeded and thinly sliced
- 1 cup blueberries
- ½ jar Loveless Cafe Blue Lightnin' Mixer
- 1 (750 ml) bottle merlot
- 2 teaspoons lemon juice

This light and festive beverage blends fresh fruit and wine with our signature Loveless Cafe Blue Lightnin' Mixer to make a sangria that's great for sippin' with friends on an autumn afternoon.

Place all fruit in a 3-quart pitcher then pour in Blue Lightnin' Mixer. Add merlot and lemon juice then mix well. Refrigerate for at least 2 hours. Serve over ice and garnish with marinated fruit.

Blue Lightnin' Punch

MAKES ¾ GALLON

- 2 lemons, thinly sliced
- 1 green apple, seeded and thinly sliced
- 2 cups blueberries
- 1 jar Loveless Cafe Blue Lightnin' Moonshine Mixer
- 1 quart lemonade
- 1 quart club soda

Use our Blue Lightnin' Moonshine Mixer as the base for this refreshing punch. It's bright, citrus flavor is perfect for family-friendly summer picnics or you can easily make an adult version with the addition of your favorite style 'shine, vodka, or gin.

Place lemons, apple, and blueberries into a 1-gallon container.

Pour Blue Lightnin' Moonshine Mixer, lemonade, and club soda into container. Mix well.

Refrigerate for at least 2 hours. Serve over ice and garnish with fruit.

DRINKS

Fruit Tea Punch

MAKES ½ GALLON

This refreshing Southern-style punch is a Nashville original that features a flavorful combination of lemon, orange, and cinnamon. Serve it as-is at any luncheon—or get creative and add some pineapple juice and dark rum to liven up the occasion. Cheers!

Pour 4 cups water into a medium saucepan and bring to a boil. Add tea bag and cinnamon stick, remove from heat, and steep for 5 to 7 minutes.

Remove cinnamon and tea bag. Add sugar and stir until dissolved. Stir in orange juice and lemonade.

Pour mixture into a large pitcher or punch bowl, add remaining 4 cups water, and stir.

Serve over ice and garnish with fresh mint or fruit.

- 8 cups water, divided
- 1 family-size tea bag
- 1 cinnamon stick
- ¾ cup sugar
- ½ cup orange juice concentrate, thawed
- ½ cup lemonade concentrate, thawed
- Sliced orange, lemon, or fresh mint for garnish (optional)

SUGGESTIONS AND ALTERNATIVES

Replace lemonade concentrate with pineapple or other fruit juice concentrate for an extra fruity variation.

To make an adult version, mix fruit tea with dark rum and garnish with orange.

Couple the cinnamon stick with 5 whole cloves and some star anise for a spiced fruit tea.

DRINKS

Countrypolitan Summer Sangria
MAKES 1½ QUARTS

The perfect summer sipper, this refreshing concoction features our popular Loveless Cafe Countrypolitan Moonshine Mixer, pinot grigio, and fresh fruit. Be sure not to toss the leftover marinated fruit once the drinks have been poured. They make a delightful adult-only snack.

Place fresh fruit into a 1-gallon pitcher then add Countrypolitan Mixer and wine. Gently stir until combined.

Refrigerate overnight.

Serve over ice and garnish with whole strawberries.

¼	cup blueberries
¼	cup fresh pineapple, cut into chunks
¼	cup apple, seeded and thinly sliced
¼	cup peaches, thinly sliced
¼	cup cantaloupe, cut into chunks
1	jar Loveless Cafe Countrypolitan Moonshine Mixer
1	(750 ml) bottle pinot grigio
	Whole strawberries (optional garnish)

DRINKS

Bacon-Infused Vodka Bloody Mary

MAKES 1 COCKTAIL

BACON-INFUSED VODKA

- 1 (750 ml) bottle vodka
- 3 strips Loveless Cafe Applewood Smoked Country Bacon, cooked and chopped

BLOODY MARY

- 2 ounces Bacon-Infused Vodka
- 6 ounces Loveless Cafe Mason Jar Mary Moonshine Mixer
- 1 strip Loveless Cafe Applewood Smoked Country Bacon, cooked (optional)
- Loveless Cafe Pickled Okra (optional)
- Fresh lemon, sliced (optional)

The sky is the limit when it comes to creative twists on the classic Bloody Mary, but we're especially fond of making ours with bacon-infused vodka. And no Bloody Mary is complete without a delectable garnish, like our Applewood Smoked Country Bacon or Pickled Okra.

MAKE BACON-INFUSED VODKA

Place bacon into a large jar and fill with vodka so that it is completely submerged. Make sure lid is closed tight. Let sit at room temperature for 12 to 24 hours before placing in freezer overnight.

Pour bacon-infused vodka into a bottle or clean jar using a funnel lined with a coffee filter to remove bacon and any fat droplets.

MAKE BLOODY MARY

Pour ice, bacon-infused vodka, and Mason Jar Mary Mixer into a shaker. Shake well. Strain into an ice-filled glass and garnish with bacon, Pickled Okra, and lemon.

HELPFUL HINTS

Rim your glass with Loveless Cafe Chicken Shake for a little extra spice!

DRINKS

Strawberry Lemonade

MAKES ½ GALLON

If you could bottle up summer and serve it over ice, it would taste just like our Strawberry Lemonade. Made with Loveless Cafe Strawberry Preserves and fresh squeezed lemon juice, this refreshing beverage is best enjoyed in a rocking chair on a front porch on a sunny afternoon.

- 9 cups water, divided
- ¾ cup sugar
- ½ cup Loveless Cafe Strawberry Preserves
- 1 cup fresh squeezed lemon juice
- Fresh sliced strawberries, lemon wedges, and mint sprigs for garnish (optional)

Pour 1 cup water and sugar into a medium saucepan. Bring to a boil and cook until sugar is dissolved, stirring occasionally. Remove from heat. Add Strawberry Preserves and mix well. Let cool for 10 minutes.

Pour cooled mixture into a 2-quart pitcher. Add lemon juice and 8 cups cold water, stirring well. Refrigerate for 2 to 3 hours.

Serve over ice and garnish with fresh strawberries, lemon, and mint.

Watermelon Punch

SERVES 12

This punch is always the life of the party! We recommend spiking it with white rum or vodka, but any clear liquor mixes great with it. Or skip the booze and pour a cup for the kiddos.

Cut watermelon in half, scoop out fruit, and place in a large bowl. Squish watermelon with both hands to break into pulp. Strain with a large sieve and extract the juice. Add sugar, salt, and orange juice to watermelon pulp. Pour mixture into a blender with ice and blend until combined. Pour into a pitcher and stir in vodka or rum.

- 1 large watermelon, refrigerated
- 2 cups sugar
- ⅛ teaspoon salt
- 1 can orange juice concentrate, thawed
- 2 cups ice, crushed
- 1½ cups white rum or vodka (optional)

Desserts

DESSERTS

Goo Goo Pie

SERVES 8

For more than a century, Goo Goo Clusters have been a Nashville culinary staple enjoyed by millions of Music City visitors. Consisting of caramel, marshmallow nougat, roasted peanuts, and a chocolate covering, Goo Goo Clusters are famously known as America's first combination candy bar. In celebration of their 100th anniversary some years ago, we created this pie which became an only-in-Nashville indulgence. That is, until you make it at home, of course!

PIE

- 3 egg whites
- 2/3 cup plus 2 tablespoons sugar
- 3/4 cup corn syrup
- 1/3 cup water
- 1 tablespoon vanilla extract
- 2 Original Goo Goo® Clusters, chopped into small pieces
- 1/4 cup roasted unsalted peanuts, chopped
- 1 (9-inch) graham cracker pie crust, baked and cooled

MAKE PIE

Pour egg whites into the bowl of a stand mixer. Add 2 tablespoons sugar and beat on low speed with wire whisk attachment just long enough to dissolve sugar. Do not allow egg whites to become frothy.

Add corn syrup and water to a heavy-bottomed pot with remaining 2/3 cup sugar. Warm over medium heat and stir to dissolve sugar. Using a pastry brush, sweep sides of pot so that no sugar crystals remain. Once sugar is dissolved, stop stirring and bring to a boil. Place a candy thermometer in pot and cook until mixture approaches 240 degrees.

When sugar is just under 240 degrees, turn stand mixer on to medium-high speed. Whip egg whites until frothy with soft peaks just beginning to form. While mixer is whipping, carefully pour hot sugar into egg whites in a steady stream. Take great care to avoid hitting beaters; hot sugar can splatter and burn. Once all hot sugar is added, add vanilla and allow egg whites to whip fully until mixture is big and fluffy, resembling marshmallow cream (approximately 1 to 2 minutes). Remove bowl from mixer and gently fold in chopped Goo Goo Cluster pieces. Set aside.

Continues on page 140

DESSERTS

Goo Goo Pie CONTINUED FROM PAGE 138

CHOCOLATE GANACHE

- 1¼ cups semisweet or dark chocolate chips
- ½ cup heavy cream

CARAMEL SAUCE

- 1 cup sugar
- ⅓ cup water
- ¾ cup heavy cream
- 2 tablespoons salted butter
- 1 teaspoon vanilla extract

MAKE CHOCOLATE GANACHE

Place chocolate chips in a medium bowl.

Simmer heavy cream in a saucepan over medium heat. Be sure not to boil. Pour heated cream over chocolate chips and let sit for 5 minutes then stir until smooth and shiny. Set aside.

MAKE CARAMEL SAUCE

Place sugar in a saucepan and shake it so it lies in an even, flat layer. Add water.

Place saucepan over medium heat and cook until sugar dissolves and turns clear (approximately 2 to 3 minutes).

Raise heat to medium-high and cook caramel until it turns amber colored (approximately 10 minutes).

Turn off heat and immediately add heavy cream.

Add butter and stir until caramel smooths out. If clumpy, turn heat back to medium and gently stir for 2 to 3 minutes until smooth. When finished cooking, add vanilla extract.

Let caramel sauce cool to room temperature then transfer to a jar and refrigerate. The sauce can be stored in refrigerator for 1 month.

PIE ASSEMBLY

Pour ¾ cup chocolate ganache into bottom of pie crust and tilt pan or use spatula to spread it evenly.

Sprinkle half the chopped peanuts evenly over ganache. Once the ganache is set, add the marshmallow pie filling.

Using an icing spreader or flat knife, decorate top of pie with remaining ganache. Sprinkle with remaining peanuts and refrigerate for at least 1 hour.

To serve, drizzle each pie slice with 2 tablespoons of caramel sauce.

DESSERTS

Peanut Butter Pie

SERVES 8

Peanut butter purists rejoice, this pie is for you! Forget jelly. Here, the lovable spread takes center stage, packing in peanutty goodness.

MAKE PIE CRUST

Blend butter, chocolate cookie crumbs, sugar, and peanuts in a medium-sized bowl.

Press mixture into a 9-inch pie plate.

MAKE PIE FILLING

Whip heavy cream until stiff peaks form. Set aside.

In a large mixing bowl, blend cream cheese and peanut butter together with an electric mixer. Add confectioners' sugar, sweetened condensed milk, and vanilla. Mix well then fold in whipped heavy cream.

Pour into prepared crust and refrigerate at least 2 hours before serving. Top pie with fresh whipped cream and garnish with chopped peanuts.

CHOCOLATE PIE CRUST

- 4½ tablespoons butter, melted
- 1 cup chocolate cookie crumbs
- 3 tablespoons sugar
- 1 tablespoon peanuts, chopped

PIE FILLING

- ½ cup heavy cream
- 4 ounces cream cheese, softened
- 1⅛ cups creamy peanut butter
- ½ cup confectioners' sugar, sifted
- ¾ cup sweetened condensed milk
- ½ teaspoon vanilla extract
- 2 tablespoons peanuts, chopped

FRESH WHIPPED CREAM

Recipe below

FRESH WHIPPED CREAM

When it comes to desserts, one thing we can't live without is fresh Whipped Cream. We always keep the ingredients for making it close by and you'll see numerous recipes in this chapter call for it. So make sure you keep this page bookmarked!

MAKES 3 CUPS

- 1⅓ cups heavy cream
- 2 tablespoons sugar
- ¼ teaspoon vanilla extract

In a chilled stand mixer bowl, combine heavy cream, sugar, and vanilla, whipping at medium speed until stiff peaks form.

Elvis Pie

SERVES 8

A pie fit for The King, this recipe transforms Elvis Presley's famously favorite sandwich into a delicious dessert. Trust us, one slice of it and you'll be all shook up!

- 5 egg yolks
- ½ cup sugar, divided
- 3 tablespoons corn starch
- 1½ cups milk
- ⅓ cup smooth peanut butter
- 3 slices Loveless Cafe Maplewood Smoked Country Bacon, cooked and chopped
- 3 ripe bananas
- 1 (9-inch) pie crust, pre-baked (see recipe on page 145)

MARSHMALLOW FLUFF

- ½ cup egg whites
- ¾ cup sugar
- 2 tablespoons corn syrup
- ½ teaspoon plain gelatin
- 1 tablespoon water, cold
- ½ teaspoon vanilla extract
- ¼ teaspoon salt

MAKE PIE

In a medium bowl, whisk egg yolks. In a second bowl, combine ¼ cup sugar with corn starch. Stir into egg yolks until smooth. Set aside.

In a saucepan, stir together milk and remaining ¼ cup sugar. Bring to a low boil over medium heat.

Slowly drizzle hot milk into the egg mixture, making sure not to cook the eggs. Return mixture to saucepan and slowly bring to a boil, stirring constantly so the eggs don't curdle or scorch on the bottom. Once mixture thickens, remove from heat and stir in peanut butter until well-blended.

Pour mixture into heat proof container and place a piece of plastic wrap directly on the surface to prevent a skin from forming. Refrigerate until chilled.

MAKE MARSHMALLOW FLUFF

In a medium bowl, combine egg whites, sugar, and corn syrup. Whisk together until blended and set aside.

In a small bowl, mix gelatin with water and let bloom (approximately 5 minutes).

In a double boiler, heat egg white mixture to 170 degrees, stirring continuously.

DESSERTS

Once mixture reaches 170 degrees, add gelatin, vanilla, and salt.

When mixture returns to 170 degrees, pour into bowl of a stand mixer and whip until stiff.

ASSEMBLY

Thinly slice bananas and lay across bottom of pie crust. Sprinkle half the bacon over bananas. Cover bacon with half the peanut butter filling. Repeat. Top with marshmallow fluff and serve.

DESSERTS

Steeplechase Pie®

SERVES 8

Add Tennessee sipping whiskey and chocolate chips to a classic pecan pie and you have a Loveless Cafe creation like no other. It's a must-eat during the Iroquois Steeplechase, a horse race held in Nashville annually since 1941 that attracts some of the world's best horses and jockeys.

- 1½ cups pecan pieces
- ½ cup semisweet chocolate chips
- 1 (9-inch) pie crust, unbaked (see recipe below)
- ¾ cup sugar
- 2 tablespoons Tennessee whiskey (such as Jack Daniel's®)
- 1 teaspoon vanilla extract
- 5½ tablespoons unsalted butter, melted
- 3 eggs
- ¾ cup light corn syrup

Preheat oven to 350 degrees.

Press pie dough into a 9-inch pie plate.

Toss pecans with chocolate chips and scatter them evenly over the bottom of pie.

Mix sugar, whiskey, and vanilla in a medium bowl. Add butter then whisk to combine. Whisk in eggs, one at a time. Add corn syrup and continue whisking until blended.

Pour mixture over nuts and chips in pie crust. Bake for 40 minutes or until the pie puffs up and sets. Let cool before serving.

EASY-AS-PIE-DOUGH

MAKES ENOUGH FOR 1 DOUBLE-CRUST 9-INCH PIE OR 2 SINGLE-CRUST PIES

- 2 cups unbleached all-purpose flour
- ½ cup confectioners' sugar
- 2 teaspoons baking powder
- ½ teaspoon salt
- ¾ unsalted butter, cold and cut into small cubes
- 2 egg yolks
- 2 tablespoons milk, cold

Place flour, confectioners' sugar, baking powder, and salt in a food processor and pulse briefly to mix. Add butter and pulse until it is cut in and mixture resembles coarse meal. Add egg yolks and milk and process just until dough is smooth and evenly moistened. Do not process until dough forms a ball or it will be tough.

Remove dough from processor, divide in half, and press each half into a ball. Flatten into two disks, wrap well, and refrigerate for at least 30 minutes before using.

DESSERTS

Homemade Peach Ice Cream

SERVES 6

It's hard to have more fun in the kitchen than making homemade ice cream. And it doesn't get more delicious than when the recipe calls for fresh, peak season peaches and Loveless Cafe Peach Preserves. This recipe uses a 2-quart ice cream maker to create a summertime classic.

- 4 fresh peaches, peeled, pitted, and chopped into bite-sized pieces
- 3 tablespoons lemon juice
- 5 egg yolks
- 1 cup light brown sugar, packed
- ½ teaspoon salt
- 4 cups whole milk
- 1 (14-ounce) can sweetened condensed milk
- 1 cup Loveless Cafe Peach Preserves
- 1 teaspoon vanilla extract

Place chopped peaches in bowl and mix in lemon juice. Once peaches have released their juices (approximately 30 minutes), mash with a pastry blender or fork.

In a large bowl, whisk together egg yolks, brown sugar, and salt until combined. Set aside.

Pour whole milk and sweetened condensed milk into a medium-sized saucepan. Heat over medium, stirring continuously. Heat milk to 170 degrees and cook for 1 minute.

Slowly add warmed milk to egg yolk mixture, stirring constantly. Return mixture to saucepan and add mashed peaches, Peach Preserves, and vanilla extract. Stir to combine.

Cook mixture over medium heat, stirring constantly, until it again reaches 170 degrees. The custard is ready when it has reduced and thickened enough that it coats the back of a spoon.

Place saucepan in sink and surround it with cold water, stirring as it cools. Pour cooled custard into a container then cover and refrigerate for at least 4 hours.

Pour custard into ice cream maker. Follow manufacturer's instructions for ice cream maker to churn.

Serve with your favorite ice cream toppings—like warmed preserves and our signature Loveless Cafe Piggy Pecans, available in our online store.

Peach Cobbler

SERVES 6 TO 8

There's lots to love about our signature cobbler. It stars the season's sweetest peaches, spiced brown sugar, and is topped with a scrumptious crust. It's the perfect ending to any summertime meal, but can be adapted all year long by substituting whatever peak season fruits are available, such as blackberries, blueberries, or mixed berries.

MAKE COBBLER

Lightly grease a 2-quart baking dish.

Mix brown sugar, pumpkin pie spice, ginger, and corn starch together in a small bowl.

Place peaches in a medium bowl then add orange juice and zest, tossing to coat peaches. Add brown sugar mixture to peaches and mix well.

Pour peaches into prepared baking dish and set aside.

MAKE DOUGH

Preheat oven to 350 degrees.

In a medium bowl, mix flour, ¾ cup sugar, baking powder, and salt. Add butter and cut into mixture until well-blended, resembling coarse meal. Add buttermilk and mix gently until sticky dough starts to form.

ASSEMBLE AND SERVE

Using a large ice cream scoop or ¼ measuring cup, drop clumps of dough over peaches, gently flattening dough with your fingertips. Sprinkle top of cobbler with 2 tablespoons sugar and bake for 45 minutes until crust is golden brown. Allow to cool for 15 minutes. Serve with a scoop of vanilla ice cream on top.

COBBLER

- ¾ cup light brown sugar
- 1½ teaspoons pumpkin pie spice
- ¾ teaspoon ginger
- ¼ cup corn starch
- 2½ pounds peaches, peeled and sliced
- ¼ cup orange juice
- Zest of 1 orange

DOUGH

- 2 cups all-purpose flour
- ½ cup sugar
- ½ tablespoon baking powder
- ½ teaspoon salt
- 1 cup unsalted butter, cold and cut into cubes
- ⅔ cup buttermilk

- 2 tablespoons sugar

DESSERTS

Coconut Cream Pie

SERVES 8

This dreamy pie is like a slice of heaven on a plate. To double the decadence, we recommend finishing it off with white chocolate shavings or garnishing with toasted coconut flakes.

PIE

- 1 (9-inch) pie crust, unbaked (see recipe on page 145)
- 1½ cups shredded coconut, toasted (plus extra for garnish)
- ½ cup plus 1 tablespoon canned coconut milk
- ⅔ cup sugar
- 1 teaspoon vanilla extract
- 2 whole eggs
- 3 large egg yolks
- ⅔ cup half-and-half
- ⅔ cup heavy cream

FRESH WHIPPED CREAM

See page 141

MAKE PIE

Preheat oven to 350 degrees.

Place pie crust in pie dish and bake for 10 to 12 minutes. Remove from oven and cool. Once cooled, spread toasted coconut in bottom of pie crust and set aside.

In a bowl, whisk together coconut milk, sugar, and vanilla.

Whisk in whole eggs. Add yolks and continue whisking. Add half-and-half and heavy cream, whisking until smooth.

Pour mixture over toasted coconut. Bake for 40 minutes, turning halfway through.

Spread fresh whipped cream evenly over cooled pie. Garnish with toasted coconut.

Apple Crumb Pie

SERVES 8

This pie is sinfully delicious and a cinch to make at home. Just fill the flaky pie crust with cinnamon and sugar–coated apples, then finish it with a crunchy oat crumb topping.

MAKE TOPPING

Place oats, flour, dark brown sugar, baking soda, cinnamon, and salt in a medium bowl. Gently mix, breaking up any lumps with your fingertips and taking care not to crush the oats.

Add butter, gently rubbing mixture together with your fingers to produce a mealy texture. Refrigerate while you prepare the apple filling.

MAKE FILLING

Preheat oven to 350 degrees.

Press pie crust into a 9-inch pie plate.

Place apple slices in a medium bowl. In another medium bowl, combine brown sugar, corn starch, and spices. Break up any lumps. Add apples and toss to coat.

Pour spiced apples into pie crust, including any sugar and juices that have accumulated in the bowl.

Sprinkle crumb topping evenly over the pie, leaving a ½-inch border uncovered. The topping will spread to cover the entire pie while baking.

Bake on middle rack for approximately 60 to 75 minutes, or until juices are bubbling and crumb topping is lightly browned all over.

OAT CRUMB TOPPING

- ½ cup rolled oats
- ½ cup all-purpose flour
- ⅓ cup dark brown sugar
- ⅛ teaspoon baking soda
- ½ teaspoon cinnamon
- ¼ teaspoon salt
- 4 tablespoons unsalted butter, cold and cut into cubes

APPLE PIE FILLING

- 1 (9-inch pie) crust, unbaked (see recipe on page 145)
- 6 cups Granny Smith apples, peeled and sliced (about 4 to 5 medium apples)
- 1 cup light brown sugar
- 2 tablespoons corn starch
- 1 teaspoon cinnamon
- 1 teaspoon apple pie spice (½ teaspoon cinnamon, ¼ teaspoon nutmeg, ¼ teaspoon allspice)

DESSERTS

Bacon Apple Pie
SERVES 8

- 1 (9-inch) pie crust, unbaked (see recipe on page 145)
- ¾ cup light brown sugar, packed
- 2 tablespoons corn starch
- 1 teaspoon cinnamon
- ½ teaspoon nutmeg
- ½ teaspoon ground cardamom
- ¼ teaspoon ground cloves
- ½ teaspoon lemon zest
- 6 cups Granny Smith apples, peeled and sliced (about 4 to 5 apples)
- 1 tablespoon fresh lemon juice
- 8 to 12 slices Loveless Cafe Applewood Smoked Country Bacon*, uncooked

*If not using our Loveless Cafe Applewood Smoked Country Bacon, be sure to use another high quality, thick-cut bacon.

Nope, that's not a typo. We really do have a delicious Bacon Apple Pie recipe for you to try at home. It features a crispy bacon lattice top rather than a traditional pie dough lattice. The result—a sweet and salty miracle!

Preheat oven to 350 degrees. Press pie crust into a 9-inch pie plate and set aside.

In a large bowl, rub brown sugar, corn starch, cinnamon, nutmeg, cardamom, cloves, and lemon zest together with fingertips until blended. Add apples to bowl and toss to coat.

Fill pie crust with apple slices, including any sugar and juices that have accumulated in the bowl.

Weave uncooked bacon over top of pie filling, starting from the center and working your way out to the edges (For a lattice topping you should have an over-under pattern with 4 to 6 pieces going vertically and 4 to 6 pieces going horizontally). Trim bacon slices to the edge of crust with scissors.

Bake on middle rack, checking after 30 minutes to make sure bacon does not burn. If bacon is browning too much, cover with foil. After 1 hour, increase oven temperature to 400 degrees. Continue baking for 15 to 25 minutes until bacon is golden brown and crisp.

Let pie cool for 1 hour before serving.

DESSERTS

Banana Pudding

SERVES 12

When we say homemade, we mean homemade. And this old-fashioned Banana Pudding recipe is no exception! You can lovingly prepare it in your kitchen the same way we've been making it at the Loveless Cafe for years.

PUDDING

- 1 cup corn starch
- 6 cups whole milk, divided
- 18 egg yolks
- ¼ vanilla bean, ends trimmed
- 2 cups plus 2 tablespoons sugar
- 2 cups fresh whipped cream
- 5 ripe bananas, sliced

HOMEMADE WAFERS

- 2 cups sugar, divided
- 6 eggs
- 3⅓ cups unbleached all-purpose flour

FRESH WHIPPED CREAM

See page 141

MAKE PUDDING

Place corn starch in a large bowl and stir in 1 cup milk until corn starch is completely dissolved. Add egg yolks and whisk together. Set aside.

Split vanilla bean and scrape seeds into a heavy-bottomed, stainless steel pot. Add sugar and remaining 5 cups milk and bring to a boil, reducing heat to prevent it from boiling over.

Ladle a small amount of hot milk mixture into whisked eggs mixture. Repeat this step until one-third of milk is mixed into the egg yolk mixture.

Pour the egg yolk mixture into the pot with remaining hot milk and return to a boil while whisking continuously for 1 minute.

Pour mixture through a sieve into a heat-proof dish, removing any lumps that may have formed.

Press plastic wrap onto the surface to prevent a skin from forming and place in refrigerator to cool.

MAKE HOMEMADE WAFERS

Preheat oven to 375 degrees. In the bowl of a stand mixer, combine 1¾ cups sugar with eggs, whipping until it forms ribbons (just before soft peaks form). Sift flour over eggs in batches, folding it in gently. Be careful not to overmix.

DESSERTS

Using a piping bag with a straight tip, pipe the batter into quarter-size wafers. Sprinkle liberally with remaining sugar and bake for 8 minutes, then rotate and bake for 8 more minutes or until completely golden to light brown. Cool and store in an airtight container.

ASSEMBLY

Spread a small amount of pudding in a dish. Top pudding with a layer of sliced bananas and then a layer of wafers. Spread more pudding over wafers to create a smooth and level surface. Repeat to fill the dish, ending with a layer of pudding. Reserve enough wafers to garnish the dish.

Wrap well and refrigerate for 6 to 8 hours or overnight. Before serving, top with whipped cream and wafers.

Jam Bars

MAKES 24 BARS

Biscuits aren't the only thing around here that we smother with Loveless Cafe Preserves. These jammin' dessert bars are easy to prepare and perfect for parties.

1	cup rolled oats (not instant oats)
1½	cups all-purpose flour
1	cup brown sugar, packed
1	teaspoon cinnamon
½	teaspoon baking soda
½	cup pecans, chopped
1	cup unsalted butter, cut into cubes
1	cup Loveless Cafe Preserves (Strawberry, Blackberry, or Peach)

Preheat oven to 375 degrees. Grease or line a 9-by-13 sheet pan with parchment paper.

Combine oats, flour, brown sugar, cinnamon, baking soda, and pecans in a mixing bowl. Add butter and mix until it forms crumbs. Measure 1½ cups of oat mixture and set aside in a small bowl.

Press remaining mixture into prepared sheet pan. Bake for 20 minutes. Allow to cool for 5 minutes. Spread preserves over crust, top with the reserved crumbs, and return to oven. Bake until top is golden brown (approximately 15 minutes).

Let cool completely then cut into bars.

DESSERTS

Cheesecake
WITH CAJUN BACON CARAMEL SAUCE

SERVES 12

With its buttery graham cracker crust and salty finish, this silky dessert makes a palate-pleasing finale to any meal.

CHEESECAKE

- 2 (8-ounce) blocks cream cheese, softened
- 3 cups graham cracker crumbs
- 1 cup sugar, divided
- 1 tablespoon ground ginger
- ½ cup unsalted butter, melted
- 2 eggs
- 1 teaspoon vanilla extract

CAJUN BACON CARAMEL SAUCE

- 3 slices Loveless Cafe Hickory Smoked Cajun Bacon
- ½ cup heavy cream
- 5 tablespoons unsalted butter, cut into cubes
- 1 cup sugar

MAKE CHEESECAKE

Preheat oven to 225 degrees. Line a 9-by-13 pan with parchment paper.

In a medium mixing bowl, combine graham cracker crumbs, ½ cup sugar, and ginger. Pour butter over graham cracker crumbs and combine well. The mixture should be thick and coarse.

Pour mixture into the parchment-lined pan. Spread evenly, using the bottom of a small measuring cup to help pack down and smooth the surface, forming a ½-inch thick crust.

With an electric mixer on medium-high speed, mix cream cheese and remaining ½ cup sugar until fluffy. Add eggs one at a time, mixing well, then add vanilla. Spread cheesecake batter onto graham cracker crust, smoothing the top.

Pour about 1 quart of water into a casserole dish and place on bottom rack of preheated oven. Place cheesecake on center rack (the water will help keep the cheesecake moist).

Bake for 2 hours. Turn off oven, open oven door, and let cheesecake rest in warm oven for 1 hour. Refrigerate for at least 1 hour while making caramel sauce.

MAKE CARAMEL SAUCE

In a cast iron skillet (or other heavy-bottom skillet), cook bacon until crispy, reserving grease in skillet. Place bacon on paper towels to drain.

Add cream and butter to bacon grease, stirring until combined. Let stand for 15 minutes. Finely chop cooled bacon.

In a second heavy-bottom skillet, heat sugar until it melts and becomes a deep amber color (approximately 10 minutes), swirling occasionally to ensure even cooking. Do not stir. Remove from heat.

Slowly add cream mixture to caramel. It will bubble dramatically at first and then subside.

Stir in chopped bacon and keep warm until ready to serve.

TO SERVE

Remove cheesecake from refrigerator, slice into squares, then drizzle with warm caramel sauce.

DESSERTS

Chess Pie

SERVES 6

It doesn't get any simpler than this Southern-pantry standby that features staple ingredients found in most kitchens. Just start with a pie crust and this timeless favorite will come to life in no time.

- 1 (9-inch) pie crust, unbaked
- 1¾ cups sugar
- 2 teaspoons vanilla extract
- 3 tablespoons yellow cornmeal
- ½ cup unsalted butter, melted
- 5 eggs
- 2 tablespoons plus 2 teaspoons heavy cream
- 2 tablespoons apple cider vinegar

Preheat oven to 350 degrees. Press pie crust into a pie plate and set aside.

Mix sugar, vanilla, and cornmeal in a medium bowl. Add butter and whisk until smooth. Whisk in eggs one at a time. Stir in heavy cream and apple cider vinegar.

Pour filling into pie crust and bake until filling is set and golden brown across the top (approximately 45 minutes). Allow pie to cool completely before serving.

Fudge Pie

SERVES 8

Our homemade Fudge Pie is rich, decadent, and sure to satisfy any sweet tooth. For a creamier pudding-like pie, take it out of the oven when the center still shimmies. Or leave it in for an additional 10 minutes for a puffier and denser pie.

MAKE PIE FILLING

Preheat oven to 350 degrees. Press pie crust into pie plate and set aside.

Heat half-and-half in a double boiler and remove from heat once it begins to simmer. Add chocolate chips and stir until smooth. Set aside to cool.

Place brown sugar in a medium bowl. Whisk in eggs, one at a time, mixing until smooth. Whisk in corn syrup.

Combine cooled chocolate mixture with egg mixture and whisk until smooth.

Pour chocolate custard into pie crust. Bake for approximately 45 minutes, turning after 20 minutes.

Remove from oven and allow to cool for 3 to 4 hours.

Mound fresh whipped cream over pie, spreading it to the edges.

MAKE CHOCOLATE SAUCE

Place chocolate chips and half-and-half in a microwave-safe dish and microwave on low heat until melted (30 to 60 seconds). Stir until smooth. Drizzle chocolate sauce over whipped cream. Serve pie immediately or refrigerate up to 2 days.

PIE FILLING

- 1 (9-inch) pie crust, partially baked
- ½ cup half-and-half
- 3 ounces unsweetened chocolate, chopped
- ⅔ cup light brown sugar, packed
- 5 eggs
- 1⅛ cups light corn syrup

FRESH WHIPPED CREAM

See page 141

CHOCOLATE SAUCE

- ¼ cup semisweet chocolate chips
- 2 tablespoons half-and-half

DESSERTS

Lemon Icebox Pie

SERVES 8

Perfect for any spring fling, this tangy pie is a delightful complement to any meal. Best part about it? Minimal cooking required!

MAKE CRUST

Place cookie crumbs, sugar, and nuts (if desired) in a bowl and stir together. Add butter and toss with a fork until evenly moistened.

Pour crumb mixture into a 9-inch pie plate. Using your fingers, pat mixture evenly across the bottom and up the sides of plate, pressing gently to pack. *Tip: Work quickly while the butter is still warm and crumbs will be much easier to manipulate.*

MAKE PIE

Preheat oven to 350 degrees.

Pour condensed milk into a medium bowl and whisk in egg yolks until completely combined. Whisk in lemon juice and zest. Pour lemon mixture into prepared crust.

Bake for 20 minutes, rotating after 10 minutes.

Allow to cool for 15 minutes. Cover with plastic wrap and refrigerate for at least 8 hours, preferably overnight.

Top pie with fresh whipped cream and your favorite garnishes.

NO-BAKE COOKIE CRUST

- 1 cup cookie crumbs (ginger snaps, graham crackers, or chocolate wafers)
- 2 tablespoons sugar
- 1 tablespoon pecans or walnuts, finely chopped (optional)
- 3 tablespoons unsalted butter, melted

PIE FILLING

- 2 (14-ounce) cans sweetened condensed milk
- 6 egg yolks
- ¾ cup fresh squeezed lemon juice
- 1¼ tablespoons lemon zest

FRESH WHIPPED CREAM

See page 141

DESSERTS

Strawberry Cupcakes
MAKES 30 CUPCAKES

These super-moist cupcakes are berrylicious and might just be the best way to enjoy the fruits at the peak of their summer season.

CUPCAKES

- 4¼ cups all-purpose flour, divided
- 2 teaspoons baking powder
- 1 teaspoon baking soda
- 1 teaspoon salt
- 1 cup whole milk
- 1 cup sour cream
- ½ cup unsalted butter, softened
- ½ cup vegetable oil
- 2 cups sugar
- 1 tablespoon vanilla
- 4 whole eggs
- 4 egg yolks
- ½ cup water
- 1½ cups strawberries, diced

STRAWBERRY PUREE

- ½ cup frozen strawberries
- ¾ tablespoon Key lime juice (or Persian lime)

MAKE CUPCAKES

Preheat oven to 350 degrees. Line muffin tins with 30 cupcake liners.

In a large bowl, sift together 4 cups flour, baking powder, baking soda, and salt. In another bowl, combine milk and sour cream, mixing well.

In the bowl of an electric mixer with paddle attachment, beat together butter, oil, sugar, and vanilla until fluffy. Add eggs and yolks, one at a time, beating well after each addition. Reduce mixer speed to low. Slowly add flour mixture and sour cream mixture, alternating between the two until well-combined. Bring ½ cup water to a boil and stir in boiling water, beating batter just until combined.

Place diced strawberries and remaining ¼ cup flour in a small bowl. Toss berries to coat. Fold strawberries into batter, stirring gently until combined.

Divide batter among lined cups, filling each three-quarters full. Bake for 20 to 25 minutes or until a toothpick inserted into the center of a cupcake comes out clean.

Place tins on wire rack and let cool before removing cupcakes. Cupcakes must be cool before they are frosted.

MAKE PUREE

Combine strawberries and lime juice in a small saucepan. Bring to simmer over medium heat. Mash strawberries with a wooden spoon and continue to simmer until berries become jam-like. Remove from heat and set aside to cool.

MAKE FROSTING AND SERVE

Place softened butter in the bowl of a stand mixer. Using the paddle attachment, beat butter on medium speed, scraping down the sides as needed, until completely smooth. Add ¼ cup of strawberry puree and beat until completely combined.

At low speed, add confectioners' sugar 1 cup at a time. Once combined, add heavy cream, vanilla, and salt. Beat on high speed until fluffy (approximately 2 minutes).

Frost cooled cupcakes and serve.

STRAWBERRY FROSTING

- 2 cups unsalted butter, softened
- 6 cups powdered sugar
- 1 tablespoon heavy cream
- 1 tablespoon vanilla extract
- ½ teaspoon salt

Key Lime Pie
SERVES 8

This classic Key Lime Pie never disappoints. The homemade graham cracker crust and pie filling come together in less than an hour for a simple, quick, and delicious dessert that will be gobbled up fast.

GRAHAM CRACKER CRUST

- 1 cup graham cracker crumbs, finely ground
- 4½ tablespoons sugar
- 5 tablespoons butter, melted

KEY LIME FILLING

- 1 whole egg
- 3 egg yolks
- 1 (14-ounce) can sweetened condensed milk
- ½ cup plus 1 tablespoon Key lime juice

MAKE GRAHAM CRACKER CRUST

Preheat oven to 350 degrees. Mix graham cracker crumbs with sugar and melted butter. Press mixture into a 9-inch pie plate. Bake for 8 minutes. Set aside to cool, leaving oven at 350 degrees.

MAKE KEY LIME PIE

In a large bowl, mix egg and yolks with sweetened condensed milk, then add Key lime juice. Pour mixture into cooled graham cracker crust.

Bake for 20 minutes at 350 degrees. Refrigerate for at least 8 hours before serving, preferably overnight.

DESSERTS

Peach Blueberry Pie

SERVES 8

This classic lattice-topped pie bursts with the flavors of summer-fresh peaches and blueberries. The sweet tartness makes it a seasonal favorite year after year.

LATTICE CRUST

- 1 cup all-purpose flour
- 6 tablespoons confectioners' sugar
- 6 tablespoons unsalted butter, cold and cut into cubes
- 1 large egg yolk

PEACH BLUEBERRY PIE

- 1 (9-inch) pie crust (see recipe on page 145)
- ½ cup sugar
- 3½ tablespoons corn starch
- ½ teaspoon lemon zest
- ½ teaspoon vanilla extract
- ¾ teaspoon pumpkin pie spice
- ½ teaspoon ground cardamom
- 1½ pounds peaches, peeled and sliced
- ¾ cup blueberries

MAKE LATTICE CRUST

Place flour and confectioners' sugar in a food processor and pulse briefly to combine. Scatter the cold butter evenly over the top of the dry ingredients. Pulse to cut in the butter, processing until no lumps are visible and the mixture is the texture of cornmeal. Add egg yolk and pulse to blend, mixing only until dough comes together. Do not over-process.

Place dough on a piece of plastic wrap and roll into a large ball. Wrap the ball in plastic wrap and refrigerate until ready to use.

MAKE PIE

Preheat oven to 350 degrees. Press pie crust into pie plate and set aside.

In a medium bowl, combine sugar, corn starch, lemon zest, vanilla, pumpkin pie spice, and cardamom. Rub mixture with your fingertips to combine thoroughly.

Add peach slices and blueberries. Toss to coat well.

Scrape the fruit, juices, and seasonings into pie crust.

On a lightly floured surface, roll out lattice dough into a disk shape approximately ¼-inch thick. With a pizza wheel or a sharp knife, cut dough into 10 strips, each about 1 inch wide. Place 1 strip over center of pie and 2 strips on either side, leaving about ½-inch between and trimming the ends to fit. Arrange remaining strips in the opposite direction on a slight diagonal to form lattice with diamond-shaped openings.

Bake for 75 minutes or until juices are bubbling gently in the center and lattice crust is golden brown. Let cool to set the filling before cutting. Serve slightly warm or at room temperature.

Bacon Pralines

MAKES 75 PRALINES

Bacon isn't just for breakfast. When used in desserts or snacks it amps up the flavor, adding just the right amount of crunch and saltiness. These classic pralines show exactly why bacon can be a dessert's best friend. This recipe is quick but precise, so make sure you have a candy thermometer on hand.

Pour 1 cup sugar in a heavy saucepan over high heat. Do not stir. Instead, tilt pan from side to side until sugar melts and turns to a dark amber color (approximately 10 minutes).

While sugar is caramelizing, combine heavy cream, remaining 4 cups sugar, and pecans in a large pot and bring to a low boil. Slowly pour caramelized sugar into cream mixture, stirring constantly. Mixture will bubble considerably.

Cook on high heat for 8 to 10 minutes, stirring occasionally, until it reaches at least 234 degrees, but no more than 240 degrees, on a candy thermometer. Stir in butter and lemon juice.

Turn off heat and stir in chopped bacon. Keep stirring slowly, until mixture starts to cool and becomes a hazy brown color.

Drop spoonfuls onto a sheet of parchment paper and let cool before serving.

- 5 cups sugar, divided
- 2 cups heavy cream
- 4 cups pecan pieces
- ½ cup butter, cut into pats
- 1 tablespoon lemon juice
- ½ pound Loveless Cafe Applewood Smoked Country Bacon, cooked crisp and finely chopped

DESSERTS

Chocolate Kahlua Bundt Cake

SERVES 6 TO 8

CAKE

- Non-stick spray
- 4 cups all-purpose flour
- 2½ cups sugar
- 2 teaspoons salt
- 2 teaspoons baking powder
- 4 teaspoons baking soda
- 1½ cups unsweetened cocoa powder
- 1 cup black coffee, cold
- 2 cups canola oil
- 1 cup Kahlua® or other coffee-flavored liqueur
- 6 eggs
- 2 teaspoons vanilla extract

GLAZE

- 1 cup coffee
- 1 cup Kahlua® or other coffee-flavored liqueur
- 2 (4-ounce) sticks salted butter
- 2 cups sugar

GARNISH

- Confectioners' sugar
- Strawberries and blackberries (optional)

Coffee and chocolate lovers, your dessert dreams have come true! The secret to making this cake almost impossibly moist? Let the Kahlua glaze soak in after baking.

MAKE CAKE

Preheat oven to 340 degrees. Spray bundt pan with oil and coat with sugar. Set aside.

In a large bowl, sift together flour, sugar, salt, baking powder, baking soda, and cocoa powder. Pour into the bowl of a stand mixer.

With paddle attachment on low speed, slowly add in coffee, oil, and Kahlua. Add eggs, one at a time, then vanilla. Mix for approximately 1 minute.

Pour batter into prepared bundt pan. Bake for 75 minutes. While cake is baking, prepare glaze.

MAKE GLAZE

In a saucepan over medium-low heat, add coffee, Kahlua, and butter. Once butter is melted, add in sugar while stirring continuously. Once mixture reaches a boil and sugar is dissolved, reduce to low heat until cake is done baking.

ASSEMBLE CAKE

Trim off top of cake with a serrated knife to make it flat. While cake is still in the bundt pan, pour all but 1 cup of the glaze over the cake and allow to soak into cake for a few minutes. Once glaze has fully soaked into cake, remove from bundt pan and pour remaining glaze on top.

Sprinkle with sifted confectioners' sugar. Garnish with fresh strawberries and blackberries.

WHITE CHOCOLATE RASPBERRY
Bread Pudding

SERVES 12

An original recipe from the Loveless Events team, this baked pudding marries raspberries, bread, and white chocolate chips to create the holy trinity of decadent desserts.

MAKE BREAD PUDDING

Preheat oven to 325 degrees. Lightly grease a 9-by-13 baking dish.

Place bread cubes in a medium bowl then set aside. In a mixing bowl, whip egg yolks, ½ cup sugar, and vanilla. Slowly add cream, whipping until color is lightened and mixture has almost doubled in size.

Slowly fold egg mixture into bread cubes, making sure not to oversoak. Pour soaked bread into prepared dish and bake for 20 minutes.

While bread cubes bake, combine egg whites and remaining ½ cup sugar in a medium bowl. Whisk or beat with a mixer until peaks form to make meringue. Set aside.

After 20 minutes, remove bread cubes from oven and let cool, about 10 minutes. Scrape bread cubes into a large bowl (do not rinse baking dish) and fold in meringue, trying not to rip the bread. Fold in white chocolate chips and berries.

Place bread pudding back into baking dish, cover with foil, and bake for 15 minutes. Remove foil and cook for an additional 10 to 15 minutes. Let cool while making glaze.

MAKE GLAZE

Heat all glaze ingredients in a double boiler until melted.

Stir and serve warm over bread pudding.

BREAD PUDDING

- 8 cups white bread (such as brioche or thick-cut toast), cubed
- 8 egg yolks (reserve whites)
- 1 cup sugar, divided
- 1½ teaspoons vanilla extract
- 3 cups heavy cream
- 8 egg whites
- 2 cups white chocolate chips
- 2 cups raspberries

WHITE CHOCOLATE GLAZE

- 2 cups white chocolate chips
- 1 cup butter
- ¼ cup heavy cream
- ¼ cup water
- 1½ teaspoons vanilla extract

DESSERTS

Red Velvet Cupcakes

MAKES 24 CUPCAKES

CUPCAKES

- 2½ cups cake flour
- ¼ cup unsweetened natural cocoa powder (Dutch processed will not rise properly)
- 1 teaspoon baking soda
- ¾ teaspoon salt
- 1½ cups sugar
- 1¼ cups canola oil
- 2 eggs
- ¼ cup red food coloring
- ¾ teaspoon distilled vinegar
- ½ tablespoon vanilla extract
- 1 cup buttermilk

CREAM CHEESE FROSTING

- 1¼ cup cream cheese, softened
- ½ cup plus 2 tablespoons unsalted butter, softened
- 5 cups confectioners' sugar, sifted
- 2 teaspoons vanilla extract

We're crazy about Red Velvet! These cupcakes are one of our February favorites—we celebrate everything Red Velvet for the entire month.

MAKE CUPCAKES

Preheat oven to 320 degrees. Place paper liners into muffin tins.

Sift flour, cocoa, baking soda, and salt into a medium bowl, whisking to combine.

In a mixing bowl, use an electric mixer on medium speed to combine sugar and canola oil until well-blended. Add eggs, one at a time, scraping the bowl as you go. Add food coloring, vinegar, and vanilla extract. Reduce mixer to low speed.

Add flour mixture to mixer bowl in batches, scraping sides of bowl and making sure batter is mixed well. Add buttermilk and scrape sides of bowl until combined.

Divide batter among lined cups, filling each three-quarters full. Bake for approximately 20 minutes, rotating tins after 10 minutes. Cupcakes are done when a toothpick inserted into the center of a cupcake comes out clean.

Place tins on wire rack and let cool before removing cupcakes.

MAKE FROSTING AND SERVE

Using an electric mixer on medium speed, combine cream cheese and butter until soft and smooth. Scrape sides of bowl to make sure everything gets mixed.

Lower mixer speed and slowly add sifted confectioners' sugar, scraping sides of bowl and beating until frosting is fluffy (approximately 3 to 5 minutes).

Cupcakes must be completely cooled before they are frosted.

Pumpkin Butter Pie

SERVES 8

Nothing says "It's fall, y'all!" louder than this seasonal pie made with Loveless Cafe Pumpkin Butter. After these slices are served, your Thanksgivings will never be the same.

MAKE PIE

Adjust oven rack to lowest position. Preheat oven to 425 degrees.

In a medium mixing bowl, combine Pumpkin Butter, pumpkin, brown sugar, spice, and salt with an electric mixer. Add eggs one at a time. Add milk slowly, mixing well.

Press pie crust into a pie plate, then pour pumpkin mixture into crust. Bake 15 minutes. Lower oven temperature to 350 degrees and bake another 35 minutes, until center is slightly puffed and jiggles when pan is tapped. Let cool on a wire rack. Leave oven on to bake garnish.

MAKE GARNISH

Preheat oven to 350 degrees. Lightly grease cookie sheet with oil.

Unroll pastry dough onto a lightly floured surface. Using a small cookie cutter, make whatever shapes you like and place on prepared cookie sheet. Beat egg with a fork then lightly brush egg on each of the garnishes.

Bake until lightly browned (approximately 5 to 7 minutes). After pie is cool, place garnishes on top and serve.

PIE

- 1 cup Loveless Cafe Pumpkin Butter
- 1 cup canned pumpkin
- ½ cup light brown sugar
- 1½ teaspoons pumpkin pie spice
- ½ teaspoon salt
- 3 eggs
- ¾ cup evaporated milk
- 1 pie crust, unbaked (see recipe on page 145)

GARNISH

- 1 sheet premade pie crust
- 1 egg

Index

Italicized page numbers indicate photos.

A

appetizers
    BBQ Bacon Deviled Eggs, 62, *63*
    BBQ-Stuffed Corn Muffins, 68, *69*
    Blackberry Bruschetta, 56, *57*
    Calico Corn Relish Dip, 58, *59*
    Chow Chow Deviled Eggs, 64, *65*
    Creamy Strawberry Preserves Dip, 67, *67*
    Hot Pepper Relish Dip, 66
    Mac n' Bacon Jalapeños, 54, *55*
    Sweet Red Pepper Cream Cheese Bites, 66
    Zesty Peach and Cream Cheese Dip, 60, *61*
apples
    Apple Cider, Hot Cranberry, 126, *127*
    Apple Crumb Pie, 149
    Bacon Apple Pie, 150, *151*

B

bacon
    Bacon Apple Pie, 150, *151*
    Bacon Balsamic-Glazed Brussels Sprouts, 110, *111*
    Bacon Cheddar Scones with Green Onions, 27
    Bacon-Infused Vodka Bloody Mary, 132, *133*
    Bacon Pralines, 163
    BBQ Bacon Deviled Eggs, 62, *63*
    Cheesecake with Cajun Bacon Caramel Sauce, 154–55, *155*
    Elvis Pie, 142–43, *143*
    Mac n' Bacon Jalapeños, 54, *55*
    Maple Bacon Pancake Muffins with Maple Cream Cheese Frosting, 30–31, *31*
    Maple Bacon Sticky Biscuits, 32–34, *33*
    Southern Turnip Greens, 108, *109*
bananas
    Banana Pudding, 152–53
    Elvis Pie, 142–43, *143*
Bars, Jam, 153
BBQ Bacon Deviled Eggs, 62, *63*
BBQ-Stuffed Corn Muffins, 68, *69*
beef
    Country Fried Steak, 95
    Meatloaf, 91
    Smoked Beef Brisket, 90
Beignets, Biscuit, 25
beverages. *See* drinks
blackberries
    Blackberry BBQ Chicken Halves, 88, *89*
    Blackberry Bruschetta, 56, *57*
    Blackberry Preserves, *43*, 44, *45*
    Blackberry Scallops, 97
Blackened Peach BBQ Salmon with Tomato Salad, 96
Black-Eyed Peas, 112
Bloody Mary, Bacon-Infused Vodka, 132, *133*

INDEX

blueberries
    Peach Blueberry Pie, 162–63
Blue Cheese Dressing, 50
Blue Lightnin' Fall Sangria, 128
Blue Lightnin' Punch, 128
Blue Ribbon Salad, *80*, *81*
bread and biscuits
    Bacon Cheddar Scones with Green Onions, 27
    Blue Cheese Biscuits, 26
    Cheddar Garlic Biscuits, 35
    Chocolate Chip Biscuits, 20, *21*
    enjoying Loveless Cafe Biscuits in person, 24
    Maple Bacon Pancake Muffins with Maple Cream Cheese Frosting, 30–31, *31*
    Maple Bacon Sticky Biscuits, 32–34, *33*
    Pumpkin Spice Biscuits, *28*, *29*
    White Chocolate Raspberry Bread Pudding, *166*, *167*
breakfast
    Bacon Cheddar Scones with Green Onions, 27
    Biscuit Beignets, 25
    Blue Cheese Biscuits, 26
    Breakfast Pizza, *22*, *23*
    Cheddar Garlic Biscuits, 35
    Chicken n' Waffles, *18*, *19*
    Chocolate Chip Biscuits, 20, *21*
    enjoying Loveless Cafe Biscuits in person, 24
    Hashbrown Casserole, *36*, *37*
    Maple Bacon Pancake Muffins with Maple Cream Cheese Frosting, 30–31, *31*
    Maple Bacon Sticky Biscuits, 32–34, *33*
    Pumpkin Spice Biscuits, *28*, *29*
    Red Eye Gravy, 38
    Red Velvet Waffles, 16, *17*
    Sausage Gravy, 39
    Sweet Potato Pancakes with Spiced Pecans and Peach Preserves Butter, 40, *41*
Brisket, Smoked Beef, 90
Brown Sugar Glazed Carrots, 104, *105*
Bruschetta, Blackberry, *56*, *57*
Brussels Sprouts, Bacon Balsamic-Glazed, *110*, *111*

C

cake
    Chocolate Kahlua Bundt Cake, 164, *165*
Calico Corn Relish Dip, 58, *59*
Caramel Sweet Potatoes, 113
Carrots, Brown Sugar, 104, *105*
Catfish, Fried, 87
Cheddar Garlic Biscuits, 35
cheese
    Bacon Cheddar Scones with Green Onions, 27
    Blue Cheese Biscuits, 26
    Blue Cheese Dressing, 50
    Breakfast Pizza, *22*, *23*
    Cheddar Garlic Biscuits, 35
    Fried Chicken Cordon Bleu, *92*, *93*
    Hashbrown Casserole, *36*, *37*
    Mac n' Bacon Jalapeños, *54*, *55*
    Pimento Cheese, *46*, *47*
    Southern Macaroni and Cheese, *106*, *107*
Cheesecake with Cajun Bacon Caramel Sauce, 154–55, *155*
Chess Pie, 156
chicken
    Blackberry BBQ Chicken Halves, *88*, *89*
    Chicken n' Dumplings, 86
    Chicken n' Waffles, *18*, *19*
    Famous Fried Chicken, *72*, *73*
    Fried Chicken Cordon Bleu, *92*, *93*
    Honey Fire Chicken, 76
    Nashville Hot Chicken, *74*, *75*
chocolate
    Chocolate Chip Biscuits, 20, *21*
    Chocolate Kahlua Bundt Cake, 164, *165*
    Fudge Pie, 157
    Goo Goo Pie, 138–40, *139*
    Steeplechase Pie, *144*, *145*
Chocolate Chip Biscuits, 20, *21*
Chow Chow Deviled Eggs, *64*, *65*
Chow Chow Potato Salad, 118
Cider, Hot Cranberry Apple, *126*, *127*
Cobbler, Peach, 147
Coconut Cream Pie, 148

INDEX

coffee
    Chocolate Kahlua Bundt Cake, *164*, *165*
    Red Eye Gravy, 38
Coleslaw, 116
Corn, Creamed, *100*, *101*
Cornbread Dressing, 119
Country Fried Steak, 95
Countrypolitan Summer Sangria, *130*, *131*
cranberries
    Cranberry Bourbon Relish, *48*, *49*
    Hot Cranberry Apple Cider, *126*, *127*
    Smoked Turkey with Cranberry BBQ Sauce, 94
Creamed Corn, *100*, *101*
Creamy Strawberry Preserves Dip, *67*, *67*
Cucumbers & Onions, *102*, *103*
cupcakes
    Red Velvet Cupcakes, 168
    Strawberry Cupcakes, 160–61

D

desserts
    Apple Crumb Pie, 149
    Bacon Apple Pie, *150*, *151*
    Bacon Pralines, 163
    Banana Pudding, 152–53
    Cheesecake with Cajun Bacon Caramel Sauce, 154-55, *155*
    Chess Pie, 156
    Chocolate Kahlua Bundt Cake, *164*, *165*
    Coconut Cream Pie, 148
    Elvis Pie, 142–43, *143*
    Fudge Pie, 157
    Goo Goo Pie, 138–40, *139*
    Homemade Peach Ice Cream, 146
    Jam Bars, 153
    Key Lime Pie, 161
    Lemon Icebox Pie, *158*, *159*
    Peach Blueberry Pie, 162–63
    Peach Cobbler, 147
    Peanut Butter Pie, 141
    Pumpkin Butter Pie, 169
    Red Velvet Cupcakes, 168
    Steeplechase Pie, *144*, 145
    Strawberry Cupcakes, 160–61
    Whipped Cream, Fresh, 141
    White Chocolate Raspberry Bread Pudding, *166*, *167*
dips
    Calico Corn Relish Dip, *58*, *59*
    Creamy Strawberry Preserves Dip, *67*, *67*
    Hot Pepper Relish Dip, 66
    Zesty Peach and Cream Cheese Dip, *60*, *61*
Dressing, Cornbread, 119
dressings
    Blue Cheese Dressing, 50
    Honey Mustard, 50
    Peach Vinaigrette, 51
    Thousand Island Dressing, 51
drinks
    Bacon-Infused Vodka Bloody Mary, *132*, *133*
    Blue Lightnin' Fall Sangria, 128
    Blue Lightnin' Punch, 128
    Classic Southern Sweet Tea, *122*, *123*
    Countrypolitan Summer Sangria, *130*, *131*
    Fruit Tea Punch, 129
    Homemade Lemonade, *124*, *125*
    Hot Cranberry Apple Cider, *126*, *127*
    Strawberry Lemonade, 134
    Watermelon Punch, 135
Drunken Pork Loin, Grilled, 77

E

eggs
    BBQ Bacon Deviled Eggs, *62*, *63*
    Breakfast Pizza, *22*, *23*
    Chow Chow Deviled Eggs, *64*, *65*
Elvis Pie, 142–43, *143*

F

fish and seafood
    Blackberry Scallops, 97
    Blackened Peach BBQ Salmon with Tomato Salad, 96
Fried Catfish, 87

INDEX

Fried Chicken, Famous, 72, 73
Fried Chicken Cordon Bleu, 92, 93
Fried Green Tomatoes, 114
Fruit Tea Punch, 129
Fudge Pie, 157

G

Goo Goo Pie, 138–40, *139*
gravy
    Red Eye Gravy, 38
    Sausage Gravy, 39
greens
    Southern Turnip Greens, 108, *109*
Grits, 117

H

ham
    Black-Eyed Peas, 112
    Fried Chicken Cordon Bleu, 92, 93
    Peach Glazed Country Ham, 84–85
    Southern Turnip Greens, 108, *109*
Hashbrown Casserole, 36, *37*
Hoe Cakes, 117
Homemade Lemonade, 124, *125*
Homemade Peach Ice Cream, 146
Honey Fire Chicken, 76
Honey Mustard, 50
Hot Cranberry Apple Cider, 126, *127*
Hot Pepper Relish Dip, 66
Hush Puppies, 115

I

Ice Cream, Homemade Peach, 146

J

Jam Bars, 153

K

Key Lime Pie, 161

L

lemonade
    Homemade Lemonade, 124, *125*
    Strawberry Lemonade, 134
Lemon Icebox Pie, *158*, 159

M

macaroni and cheese
    Mac n' Bacon Jalapeños, 54, *55*
    Southern Macaroni and Cheese, 106, *107*
main dishes
    Blackberry BBQ Chicken Halves, *88*, 89
    Blackberry Scallops, 97
    Blackened Peach BBQ Salmon with Tomato Salad, 96
    Blue Ribbon Salad, 80, *81*
    Chicken n' Dumplings, 86
    Country Fried Steak, 95
    Famous Fried Chicken, 72, *73*
    Fried Chicken Cordon Bleu, 92, *93*
    Grilled Drunken Pork Loin, 77
    Honey Fire Chicken, 76
    Meatloaf, 91
    Nashville Hot Chicken, *74*, 75
    Peach Glazed Country Ham, 84–85
    Peach Glazed Pork Chops, 82–83, *83*
    Smoked Beef Brisket, 90
    Smoked Turkey with Cranberry BBQ Sauce, 94
    Watermelon Ribs, 78, *79*
maple syrup
    Maple Bacon Pancake Muffins with Maple Cream Cheese Frosting, 30–31, *31*
    Maple Bacon Sticky Biscuits, 32–34, *33*
Meatloaf, 91
muffins
    BBQ-Stuffed Corn Muffins, 68, *69*
    Maple Bacon Pancake Muffins with Maple Cream Cheese Frosting, 30–31, *31*

M

Nashville Hot Chicken, *74*, 75
nuts
    Bacon Pralines, 163
    Steeplechase Pie, *144*, 145

INDEX

Sweet Potato Pancakes with Spiced Pecans and Peach Preserves Butter, 40, *41*

P

pancakes
    Sweet Potato Pancakes with Spiced Pecans and Peach Preserves Butter, 40, *41*
peach(es)
    Blackened Peach BBQ Salmon with Tomato Salad, 96
    Homemade Peach Ice Cream, 146
    Peach Blueberry Pie, 162–63
    Peach Cobbler, 147
    Peach Glazed Country Ham, 84–85
    Peach Glazed Pork Chops, 82–83, *83*
    Peach Preserves, 44
    Peach Vinaigrette, 51
    Zesty Peach and Cream Cheese Dip, 60, *61*
peanut butter
    Elvis Pie, 142–43, *143*
    Peanut Butter Pie, 141
pecans
    Bacon Pralines, 163
    Steeplechase Pie, *144*, 145
    Sweet Potato Pancakes with Spiced Pecans and Peach Preserves Butter, 40, *41*
pie
    Apple Crumb Pie, 149
    Bacon Apple Pie, 150, *151*
    Chess Pie, 156
    Coconut Cream Pie, 148
    Elvis Pie, 142–43, *143*
    Fudge Pie, 157
    Goo Goo Pie, 138–40, *139*
    Key Lime Pie, 161
    Lemon Icebox Pie, *158*, 159
    Peach Blueberry Pie, 162–63
    Peanut Butter Pie, 141
    Pumpkin Butter Pie, 169
    Steeplechase Pie, *144*, 145
Pimento Cheese, 46, *47*
Pizza, Breakfast, 22, 23

pork
    BBQ-Stuffed Corn Muffins, 68, *69*
    Grilled Drunken Pork Loin, 77
    Peach Glazed Pork Chops, 82–83, *83*
    Watermelon Ribs, 78, *79*
potatoes
    Chow Chow Potato Salad, 118
    Hashbrown Casserole, 36, *37*
Pralines, Bacon, 163
preserves and spreads
    Blackberry Preserves, *43*, 44, *45*
    Cranberry Bourbon Relish, *48*, 49
    Jam Bars, 153
    Peach Preserves, *43*, 44
    Pimento Cheese, 46, *47*
    Strawberry Preserves, *43*, 44
Pudding, Banana, 152–53
Pumpkin Butter Pie, 169
Pumpkin Spice Biscuits, *28*, 29
punch
    Blue Lightnin' Punch, 128
    Fruit Tea Punch, 129
    Watermelon Punch, 135

R

raspberries
    White Chocolate Raspberry Bread Pudding, *166*, 167
Red Eye Gravy, 38
red velvet
    Red Velvet Cupcakes, 168
    Red Velvet Waffles, 16, *17*
relish
    Calico Corn Relish Dip, 58, *59*
    Chow Chow Deviled Eggs, 64, *65*
    Chow Chow Potato Salad, 118
    Cranberry Bourbon Relish, *48*, 49
    Hot Pepper Relish Dip, 66
    Sweet Red Pepper Cream Cheese Bites, 66
Ribs, Watermelon, 78, *79*

INDEX

S

salads
- Blue Ribbon Salad, *80, 81*
- Chow Chow Potato Salad, *118*
- Coleslaw, *116*
- Cucumbers & Onions, *102, 103*
- Tomato Salad, Blackened Peach BBQ Salmon with, *96*

sangria
- Blue Lightnin' Fall Sangria, *128*
- Countrypolitan Summer Sangria, *130, 131*

Sausage Gravy, *39*

scones
- Bacon Cheddar Scones with Green Onions, *27*

side dishes
- Bacon Balsamic-Glazed Brussels Sprouts, *110, 111*
- Black-Eyed Peas, *112*
- Brown Sugar Glazed Carrots, *104, 105*
- Caramel Sweet Potatoes, *113*
- Chow Chow Potato Salad, *118*
- Coleslaw, *116*
- Cornbread Dressing, *119*
- Creamed Corn, *100, 101*
- Cucumbers & Onions, *102, 103*
- Fried Green Tomatoes, *114*
- Grits, *117*
- Hoe Cakes, *117*
- Hush Puppies, *115*
- Southern Macaroni and Cheese, *106, 107*
- Southern Turnip Greens, *108, 109*

Smoked Beef Brisket, *90*
Smoked Turkey with Cranberry BBQ Sauce, *94*
Southern Macaroni and Cheese, *106, 107*
Southern Sweet Tea, Classic, *122, 123*
Southern Turnip Greens, *108, 109*
Steeplechase Pie, *144, 145*

strawberries
- Creamy Strawberry Preserves Dip, *67, 67*
- Strawberry Cupcakes, *160–61*
- Strawberry Lemonade, *134*
- Strawberry Preserves, *43, 44*

sweet potatoes
- Caramel Sweet Potatoes, *113*
- Sweet Potato Pancakes with Spiced Pecans and Peach Preserves Butter, *40, 41*

Sweet Red Pepper Cream Cheese Bites, *66*
Sweet Tea, Classic Southern, *122, 123*

T

Thousand Island Dressing, *51*
Tomatoes, Fried Green, *114*

turkey
- Smoked Turkey with Cranberry BBQ Sauce, *94*

Turnip Greens, Southern, *108, 109*

W

waffles
- Chicken n' Waffles, *18, 19*
- Red Velvet Waffles, *16, 17*

watermelon
- Watermelon Punch, *135*
- Watermelon Ribs, *78, 79*

Whipped Cream, Fresh, *141*
White Chocolate Raspberry Bread Pudding, *166, 167*

Z

Zesty Peach and Cream Cheese Dip, *60, 61*